The

CAT

ENCYCLOPEDIA

for KIDS

by
Joanne Mattern

Capstone Young Readers
a capstone imprint

Table of Contents

Introduction

People and cats go way back. Judging by the paintings, sculptures, and even mummies left behind, we know that ancient Egyptian people were fond of cats. But some archaeologists have found evidence dating back 9,500 years, indicating cats may have become **domesticated** in Cyprus long before. There are some scientists who believe that this human-cat relationship may have an even longer history. These scientists did genetic testing that indicated domestication of cats might have begun closer to 12,000 years ago.

Scientists and historians have different theories about how cats became domesticated. A popular theory is that people captured cats to help control rodent populations in their homes and on their farms. The warmth, food, and shelter they were given in return encouraged cats to stick around.

The history of breeding is also complex. Humans probably bred these rodent-killing cats to be tamer than cats in the wild. People also might have begun breeding cats to produce new species with clear physical and behavioral **traits**. This kind of cat breeding is thought to date back as far as 4,000 years in ancient Egypt.

Today there are 42 distinct cat **breeds** recognized by the Cat Fanciers' Association (CFA). These cat breeds each have a **breed standard** defined by the organization, which indicates the physical features of each breed that a judge looks for in a cat show. The CFA, which was founded in 1906, is currently the largest **registry** of **pedigreed** cats.

Get ready to discover twelve of the most popular cat breeds, including Abyssinian, American Shorthair, Birman, Exotic, Maine Coon, Manx, Ocicat, Oriental, Persian, Ragdoll, Siamese, and Sphynx. Discover each breed's size and appearance, personality and behaviors, breed history, and care tips. You'll learn which cat might be best suited for you and your family, and you'll be equipped with everything you need to know to become a successful cat owner!

Some words are bolded, **like this**. You can find out what they mean on pages 204–205.

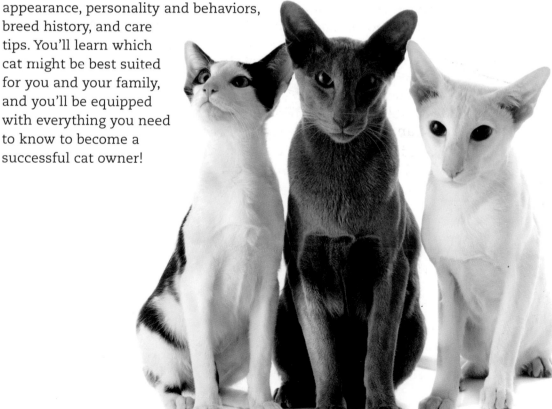

Abyssinian

When people see Abyssinian (AB-uh-SIN-ee-uhn) cats for the first time, they often say how much the cats look like small wildcats. Abyssinians' soft, sleek fur has an **agouti** pattern. This coat pattern has bands of light and dark color on each hair. Agouti coats are sometimes called **ticked** coats. They are also seen in wildcats such as cougars and lions.

Abyssinians are active, intelligent, and friendly. People often call them "Abys" for short. These cats seem to enjoy being around people. They usually stay close to their owners, trying to be involved in whatever the owner is doing.

In 2016 the CFA ranked the Abyssinian as the ninth most popular breed.

FUN FACT: Abys' agouti coats set them apart from other cat breeds.

Abyssinian History

The Abyssinian is one of the oldest cat breeds. No one knows exactly where or when the Abyssinian breed began. Some people think that these cats lived in the palaces of the ancient Egyptian pharaohs. These kings ruled Egypt thousands of years ago. Mummified cats have been discovered in ancient Egyptian tombs.

Statues and drawings of cats found in Egyptian tombs look much like today's Abyssinians. The cats in this artwork also have slender bodies, heads shaped like **wedges**, and large eyes. But these features are also found in the Siamese and Oriental breeds. No one can prove exactly what kind of cat lived in ancient Egypt.

FUN FACT: Two silver Abys named Aluminum and Salt were the first of their breed to come to the United States.

Ancient Egyptian cat statues look
much like today's Abyssinians.

Zula

The Abyssinian gets its name from the African region of Abyssinia. Today this area is part of the country of Ethiopia.

During the 1860s Great Britain fought a war in Abyssinia. In 1868 a British Army officer brought a cat named Zula from Abyssinia to Britain. Zula had an agouti coat, but otherwise she didn't look like today's Abys. Still, some people believe Zula may have been the founder of the Abyssinian breed.

Others think the breed began in Great Britain. British breeders crossed striped silver and brown **tabby** cats with "bunny" cats **native** to Great Britain. The bunny cats' fur color was similar to that of rabbit fur. Traders may also have brought Abyssinians from Southeast Asia when they traveled to Britain.

Great Britain's National Cat Club registered its first Abyssinians in 1896. British breeders exhibited a few Abyssinians in cat shows during the late 1800s.

FUN FACT:
Abyssinians were known as British Ticks in the early 1900s.

Modern Abys

The early 1900s were difficult for the Abyssinian breed. Great Britain and other European nations were involved in World War I (1914–1918) and World War II (1939–1945). Most people did not have the time or money to breed cats during the war years. The Abyssinian breed almost disappeared in Europe. They didn't reach large numbers again until the 1960s.

During the early 1900s, some breeders brought Abyssinian cats to North America from Europe. But the breed developed slowly and did not become popular in North America until the 1930s. At that time, breeders brought several Abyssinians from Great Britain to the United States.

By the 1950s, many North American breeders were raising Abyssinians. Today the Abyssinian is more popular in North America than it is in Europe.

Modern Abys' ticked markings may have come from cats native to Great Britain.

Abyssinians are one of the most playful cat breeds.

FUN FACT: Many Abys seem to enjoy water. They may play with water that drips from faucets or even jump in a filled bathtub!

Abyssinian Traits

Red Aby

Abyssinians are average in size compared to other cats. Adult Abys weigh 7 to 12 pounds (3.2 to 5.4 kilograms). Females are usually slightly smaller than males.

Body

Abys are long, slim, and muscular. Their slender legs are ideal for running and jumping. Their tails are long and thin. Their short, thick fur is soft and shiny.

An Aby's head is wedge-shaped. Its ears are large, pointed, and alert. An Aby's large eyes can be green, gold, copper, or **hazel**. The eyes have a thin, dark ring around the eyelids.

Colors

The original Abyssinian coat color was **ruddy**. This coat is dark brown with black ticking. Over the years, breeders have developed other colors. Red Abys have orange-red fur with brown ticking. Blue Abys are light blue-gray with darker blue-gray ticking. **Fawn** Abys have light pink-beige fur with brown ticking.

Breeders also have developed silver, chocolate, and lilac Abys. Silver Abys have silver coats with black ticking. Chocolate Abys are a medium brown color with black ticking. Lilac Abys have pink-gray coats with darker pink-gray ticking. These colors are rare. Abyssinians of these colors can't compete in most cat shows.

Other features can prevent an Abyssinian from being exhibited in cat shows. One is white fur on any part of the body except around the nose, chin, and upper throat. Another is a reverse ticking pattern in the coat. Cats with this ticking pattern have darker coats with lighter ticking. But Abyssinians that are not of show quality still make good pets.

Personality

Abyssinians' wild look and friendly personality makes them great additions to many families.

Abyssinians are one of the most active, sociable cat breeds. Some people say the Aby's personality is more like a dog than a cat. Some Abys even learn to walk on leashes, do tricks, and play fetch or other games.

Abys are always curious about their surroundings. When the doorbell rings, they run to see who is there. If their owners are doing something, they want to be right in the middle of it.

Abys may be active and playful, but their meows are soft and low.

FUN FACT: Cats that aren't tame rarely meow. Experts believe tame cats meow to communicate with the humans in their lives.

Abys are vocal, but their meows aren't loud.

Abys are devoted and loyal friends to their owners.

Caring for an Abyssinian

Health Care

Most Abyssinians are healthy. But some Abys will develop **renal amyloidosis**, an inherited disease that causes kidney failure and death. Other cat breeds also can get this disease. If you get your Aby from a breeder, ask the breeder if there is any history of this disease in your cat's family.

In general, Abyssinian cats are very healthy. Owners who provide good care for their Abys can expect their cats to live 15 to 20 years.

Dental Care

All cats need regular dental care to protect their teeth and gums from **plaque**. Dental care is especially important for Abys because they are more likely to develop **gingivitis** than other breeds. Brush your Aby's teeth at least once a week with a toothbrush made for cats or a soft cloth. Be sure to use toothpaste made for cats.

Grooming

An Abyssinian's short, sleek coat requires little care. An occasional brushing will remove loose hair. You can also gently rub your Aby's coat with a damp cloth to keep it shiny.

Is an Aby Right for You?

Abys are natural athletes. They run, jump, and climb. Owners often find them sitting in high places such as the tops of bookcases or refrigerators. They also are more playful than many cat breeds. Many cats are less playful as they age. But Abys seem to enjoy playing throughout their lives.

The Abyssinian's friendly, playful nature makes it an especially good family pet. Abys get along well with dogs and most other cats. But Abys are also one of the most active cat breeds. If you prefer a cat that sits quietly most of the day, an Aby isn't for you.

People who want a show-quality Abyssinian should buy one from a breeder. An owner who buys a kitten from a breeder often can meet the kitten's parents. This gives the owner an idea of how the kitten will look and behave as an adult.

Breed rescue organizations can be a less expensive way to adopt an Aby. Organization members care for unwanted or neglected animals. They try to find new owners for the animals. Pets from breed rescue groups usually are **purebred**. They may even be registered.

Abyssinians tend to have only three or four kittens per **litter**. More males are born than females, so there are fewer female cats to produce kittens. These facts can make Abyssinians more expensive than other cat breeds.

FUN FACT: Most experts believe cats see in color, so brightly colored toys may especially appeal to your cat.

Abys have muscular, lean bodies.

American Shorthair

The American Shorthair is one of North America's oldest cat breeds. These cats have calm, affectionate personalities. They enjoy being around people and have no problem jumping into your lap for attention. They love to get exercise and play with cat toys. American Shorthairs also tend to be healthy and rarely need special care. Because of their short coats, they tend not to shed as much as some other cat breeds.

These qualities make the breed one of the most popular in North America. In 2016 the American Shorthair was the sixth most popular breed in the CFA.

FUN FACT: American Shorthairs are "four-on-the-floor" cats, meaning they would rather get around on their own than be carried.

An American Shorthair's wide eyes and round face give it a friendly appearance.

American Shorthair History

The American Shorthair is one of the few cat breeds that developed in North America. Shorthaired cats came to the continent with early explorers and settlers from Europe. The cats, often called **mousers**, caught rats and mice on the ships.

Many historians believe the Pilgrims brought cats aboard the Mayflower. The American Shorthair breed is a **descendant** of these early North American cats.

A New Breed

Early European settlers in North America used shorthaired cats to rid their houses and barns of rats and mice. In the late 1800s, they wanted cats for a different reason. People became interested in breeding and showing cats.

Around this time, Siamese and some longhaired breeds were brought to North America from Europe and Asia. These cats were sometimes allowed to run free and mate with native shorthaired cats. The resulting kittens often looked much different from the shorthaired cats.

Some people wanted to preserve the native shorthaired breed. They chose shorthaired cats with the best qualities, such as a tough coat, and began to breed them. They called the breed the Shorthair. Later, the breed's name was changed to the Domestic Shorthair.

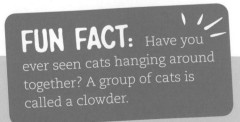

FUN FACT: Have you ever seen cats hanging around together? A group of cats is called a clowder.

The first Shorthairs were nicknamed "mousers" because of their ability to catch mice.

Some cats perform tricks and routines at cat shows.

Gaining Respect

In 1906 the CFA included the Domestic Shorthair as one of the first five recognized cat breeds. For many years, the CFA's recognition didn't help the Domestic Shorthair's popularity. The cats received little respect and attention from cat show judges and breeders. They preferred breeds from other countries, such as the Persian and the Siamese. Domestic Shorthairs could only compete in the household pets class at many cat shows. Cat clubs often did not provide cages or trophies for Domestic Shorthairs at cat shows.

The Domestic Shorthair breed began to gain respect during the 1960s. In 1964 a silver cat named Shawnee Sixth Son won the CFA's Kitten of the Year award. Shawnee won another award, Cat of the Year, the following year.

In 1966 breeders voted to change the breed's name from Domestic Shorthair to American Shorthair. The name was changed to reflect the breed's history in North America. Today the American Shorthair is known as a truly American cat.

You may still hear the term Domestic Shorthair today. Not to be confused with purebred American Shorthairs, Domestic Shorthairs are often thought to be the feline equivalent of a mutt — meaning their ancestry is often not known or is of mixed breeds. "Domestic Shorthair" is what many call shorthaired cats of mixed-breed ancestry. "Domestic Longhair" is used to describe longhaired mixed-breed cats. Domestic Shorthairs are very common household pets.

FUN FACT: More than 100 years ago, an American Shorthair was priced at $2,500 at a cat show. That's equal to about $63,000 today!

American Shorthair Traits

American Shorthairs are medium-sized cats. Males usually weigh between 11 and 15 pounds (5 and 6.8 kg). Females are smaller. They usually weigh between 8 and 12 pounds (3.6 and 5.4 kg).

Most cat breeds are fully grown at one year. But American Shorthairs may not reach their full size until they are three or four years old.

Body

The American Shorthair has a muscular, sturdy body. Its coat is made up of short, thick fur that feels dense to the touch. A Shorthair's legs and neck are muscular, but they are average in size compared to other cats. Its tail is medium to long in length. The tail is thick at the base and thinner at the tip. A Shorthair's broad back helps the playful breed stay active.

The American Shorthair breed is known for having large eyes, a wide head, and round cheeks. It has an average-sized nose, and its mouth is filled with strong teeth for catching **prey**.

FUN FACT:

American Shorthairs' coats can be one of more than 80 combinations of colors and patterns.

American Shorthairs come in a variety
of colors and patterns.

Silver Tabby

Colors

Some American Shorthair cats are only one solid color. Others have patches and markings of two or more colors. These colors include white, blue, red, and silver. Blue is a shade of gray. Red is a shade of orange.

The coats of calico cats have a blend of three colors.

Silver tabby is the most common American Shorthair color pattern. These cats have silver coats with black striped markings. They have a black marking on their foreheads that looks like the letter "M." Red tabby is another common color pattern among American Shorthairs. These cats have medium-orange fur with darker orange tabby markings.

Bi-color, smoke, and **van** patterns are also found in American Shorthairs. Bi-colors have patches of white and a solid color. Smoke cats have a white undercoat with an overcoat of another solid color. Vans have white coats with patches of a different color on their head, tail, and legs.

American Shorthairs may also be calico or tortoiseshell. Calico cats' coats have large patches of three colors. The most common colors are white and shades of black and red. Tortoiseshells' coats are a mixture of red, black, and white fur.

FUN FACT: Nearly all calico and tortoiseshell cats are female, and most red or orange tabbies are male.

American Shorthairs open their mouths
to meow, but often no sound comes out.

Personality

American Shorthairs have become increasingly popular as family pets. Their playful nature and caring attitude make them welcome in many homes. They are known for getting along well with children, other cats, and even dogs. They do not seem to enjoy being alone. For this reason, many American Shorthair owners who are not at home during the day own two or more cats.

American Shorthairs are affectionate and friendly. They often follow their owners from room to room. They may sit near their owners for hours.

These cats are lively. They like to spend time playing with cat toys. They often enjoy chasing balls or crumpled pieces of paper. Unlike some cat breeds that are known to be playful only as kittens, American Shorthairs remain frisky throughout their lives.

American Shorthairs are intelligent as well. Owners often can train their American Shorthairs to fetch toys or other objects.

Although they are playful, American Shorthairs are known as a quiet breed. These cats seldom meow unless they are hungry. Their meow is soft and low.

American Shorthairs love to play with toys.

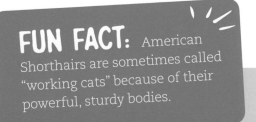

FUN FACT: American Shorthairs are sometimes called "working cats" because of their powerful, sturdy bodies.

Caring for an American Shorthair

Grooming

American Shorthairs need little grooming compared to longhaired breeds. American Shorthairs should be brushed at least once each week with a soft bristle brush to remove loose hair. After brushing, you should use a coarse comb to smooth out the cat's fur. Be careful when you brush and comb an American Shorthair. If you press too hard, the bristles may break off pieces of fur. They can also scrape the cat's skin.

Health Care

Although most American Shorthairs have few health problems, some tend to overeat. **Overweight** cats are at greater risk for health problems such as **diabetes**. This serious disease is caused when the cat's body does not produce a substance called **insulin**. The cat's body cannot store sugar or convert it to energy. Cats that have diabetes will die unless they receive regular shots of insulin.

Generally a strong and healthy breed, American Shorthair cats often live 15 to 20 years. People who choose them as pets should be ready for a long-term commitment to their cat.

FUN FACT: Cats spend one-third of their lives grooming themselves. This natural behavior keeps them clean, healthy, and comfortable.

Today's American Shorthairs are the result of
careful breeding more than a century ago.

Is an American Shorthair Right for You?

If you're looking for a good-natured, affectionate cat to call your own, the American Shorthair makes a great family pet. These cats are loyal companions that tend to enjoy the company of children and dogs.

People who want to own an American Shorthair can buy one from a quality breeder. Breeders make sure their cats are healthy. A breeder usually owns one or both of the kitten's parents. Many owners like to meet the kitten's parents. They can learn how the kitten might look and behave when it is grown.

You can also try to adopt an American Shorthair at your local animal shelter, though purebred cats may be hard to find. The cat's medical history might not be known at an animal shelter. Still, it can be an inexpensive place to get a lovable pet who needs a home.

American Shorthairs are playful and enjoy being near people.

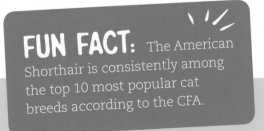

FUN FACT: The American Shorthair is consistently among the top 10 most popular cat breeds according to the CFA.

Birman

With a look and personality all their own, Birmans stand out in the cat world. They make unique feline friends for many individuals and families.

Birman cats are known as the "sacred cats of Burma." Birmans got this nickname because the cats may have once lived in temples with Birman priests. The priests are thought to have treasured the good-natured cats as loyal pets.

Modern Birman owners also treasure their cats. Many people like Birmans because they are calm and affectionate. People also value the breed's unique look. Long fur, bold **colorpoints**, and pure white paws set the Birman apart from other breeds.

FUN FACT: The Birman name comes from *Birmanie*. This word is the French spelling for "Burma."

The Birman's pure white paws make it unique
from other breeds with colorpoints.

Birman History

No clear record of the Birman's origin exists. But there is one popular legend that describes how the Birman got its coloring. A priest named Mun-Ha lived in the temple of Lao-Tsun. People worshipped a blue-eyed goddess named Tsun-Kyan-Kse at this temple. White longhaired cats with yellow eyes helped guard the temple. The temple's head priest, Mun-Ha, had a cat named Sihn.

One day thieves attacked the temple. They killed Mun-Ha in front of a golden statue of Tsun-Kyan-Kse. Sihn placed his feet on his master and faced the golden statue. Sihn's white fur then took on a golden glow. His face, ears, legs, and tail turned dark brown to match the earth. But Sihn's paws turned white where they touched Mun-Ha's head. Sihn's eyes also turned from yellow to dark blue.

The legend says that Mun-Ha's soul left his body and entered Sihn. The cat stayed by his dead master's body for seven days before he also died.

Some people believed Sihn carried Mun-Ha's soul to heaven when he died. After Sihn's death, the coats and eye color of the other cats in the temple changed in the same way. The legend says that each cat carries the soul of a priest on his journey to the afterlife.

FUN FACT:
According to the legend, Sihn's white paws represent purity.

A legend explains how the Birman got its blue eyes and the golden mist on its coat.

More Mysteries

The origin of the first Birman cats in Europe is as mysterious as the origin of the breed. No one is really sure when the first Birman cats came to Europe. One story says that two Englishmen helped Burmese priests protect their temple during World War I (1914–1918). The men were Major Gordon Russell and August Pavie. To show their thanks, the priests sent a pair of Birmans to the men while they were living in France.

Another story says that a wealthy American received a pair of Birman cats from a temple servant in Burma. The man's full name is not known, but the story says his last name was Vanderbilt. Mr. Vanderbilt then sent the cats to a friend in France.

Beyond the Legends

While many stories exist, there are a few generally accepted facts about the Birman's history in Europe. Someone in Burma sent a pair of Birman cats to another person in France in 1919. The male Birman was named Maldapour. The female cat was named Sita. Maldapour did not survive the long journey. But Sita gave birth to kittens when she arrived in France.

One kitten was named Poupee. Many people believe Poupee was bred to a Siamese cat. Siamese cats have colorpoints like Birmans do. In 1925 French cat associations recognized Birmans.

FUN FACT: Most U.S. Birman breeders follow a French tradition of naming their cats. They give all kittens born in the same year names that begin with the same letter.

The golden mist of Birmans ranges in shade. Cats with very dark colorpoints often have a deep golden glow.

The Birman breed almost died out in Europe during World War II (1939–1945). Many people believe only two Birmans were alive at the end of the war. These cats were bred to Persians and cats of other breeds. This **crossbreeding** allowed the Birman traits to continue. Even though these Birmans were crossbred, people still considered them to be Birmans.

Birmans in the United States

The first Birman cats probably arrived in the United States in 1959. In 1961 cat breeder Gertrude Griswold received two colorpointed cats as a gift. She later discovered that the cats were Birmans. She arranged to breed these cats with Birmans from France. Griswold's breeding program helped build interest in Birman cats in the United States.

Other North American breeders soon bought Birmans from breeders in England and France. In 1967 the CFA recognized the breed. Five years later, a cat named Griswold's Romar of Bybee became the first Birman to win a CFA Grand Champion title. Over time the Birman breed gained popularity in North America.

FUN FACT: A Birman first received a CFA National Winner title in the 1988–1989 show season. National Winner titles are given to the highest scoring cats of a show season.

Owners make sure their Birmans are clean
and expertly groomed for shows.

Birman Traits

Birmans are medium-sized cats. Males can weigh as much as 14 pounds (6.4 kg). Females can weigh up to 11 pounds (5 kg). A Birman's long body is sturdy and muscular. Birmans have thick legs, round paws, and a medium-length tail.

Colors

Birman cats have four traditional coat colors. These colors are seal point, blue point, chocolate point, and lilac point. The four colors are called traditional because they naturally occur in the breed. **Seal-point** Birmans have ivory coats with dark brown points. The points on some seal-point Birmans look almost black.

Chocolate-point Birmans have ivory coats with light brown points. Dark blue-gray points mark blue-point Birmans. These cats have blue-white to pale ivory coats. Lilac-point Birmans have off-white coats and light pink-gray points.

In the CFA, the ideal Birman coat color has a slight golden tone. The misty golden color often appears on a cat's sides and back.

Some breeders have mated Birmans to cats of other breeds. This crossbreeding has produced colors other than the traditional ones. Today's Birmans can have a variety of colors and patterns. Lynx-point cats have lightly striped coats and more heavily striped points. Other Birmans have cream bodies and deep red points. Tortie-point Birmans have brown points with a mix of another color such as red or cream.

FUN FACT: Birmans may take three years to fully develop. Many other cat breeds are fully grown after one year.

A Tortie-point Birman

What Causes Colorpoints?

Colorpoints are produced by a **gene** in Birman cats. This special gene is heat sensitive. Cool parts of the Birman body have dark fur. These body parts include the ears, tail, and face. Warm parts of the Birman body have lighter-colored fur. Birman kittens are born white. Their points begin to appear when they are a few days old. Dark-colored Birmans such as seal points often develop their colorpoints earlier than light-colored Birmans do.

Markings

One of a Birman's most noticeable features is its white paw markings, or gloves. The gloves on the back feet extend up the back of the legs. These markings are called laces.

In the CFA, Birmans' gloves and laces should look a certain way for competition. The gloves should stretch across each paw in an even line. The laces should end in a point on the back of the cats' legs. Laces should also line up evenly. It is rare for a Birman to have ideal gloves and laces on all four feet.

FUN FACT: Seal-point Birmans often have a darker golden mist on their coats than Birmans of other colors.

A Birman with gloves that extend evenly across all four paws is likely to receive high scores at cat shows.

Birman kittens are often more playful than adults.

Coats

The Birman's thick, long coat is silky to the touch. Many Birmans have a heavy **ruff** and slightly curly hair on their stomachs.

Facial Features

Birmans have wide, round heads with a slight flat spot in front of the ears. The ears are set wide apart and are slightly rounded at the tips. The Birman's chin is well developed and its cheeks are full.

A Birman's blue eyes are also wide set. The eye color shade varies. In show cats, the CFA prefers a deep, bright blue color.

Personality

Many people think the Birman is an ideal companion. Birmans are not as active as some shorthaired breeds or as inactive as some other longhaired breeds.

Birmans usually are very calm. They often quietly watch the activities of people and other animals without interrupting. Because of these actions, many people describe the Birman as a polite cat.

A Birman's blue eyes are almost perfectly round.

FUN FACT: Some people believe crossbreeding with the Angora cat played a role in giving the Birman its long hair.

Caring for a Birman

Grooming

Birmans' coats are easier to care for than coats of other longhaired breeds. But Birmans should still be brushed weekly. A natural bristle brush is best to use. A comb works well on thick areas of the coat. You will need to brush your Birman more often in spring when its winter coat is shedding.

Some owners bathe their Birmans occasionally. Bathing can help remove loose hair and keep the cats' coats clean. If you bathe your cat, use a shampoo made for cats.

Health Care

Birman cats generally have few health problems. The most common problem is **hairballs**. Many longhaired cats have hairballs at some time in their lives. Large hairballs can become trapped in a cat's digestive system. A vet may have to remove these hairballs. Regular brushing is the best way to prevent hairballs in Birmans.

Is a Birman Right for You?

Birmans make good family pets. These friendly, gentle cats seem to enjoy being around people and other animals. Birmans get along well with dogs and most other cats. They do not seem to like being alone. Owners should have other pets in the house if no people are at home during the day.

You can find a Birman in one of several ways. Visiting a breeder is one of the best ways to find a Birman. You may also be able to find a Birman through a breed rescue organization or an animal shelter.

FUN FACT: The oldest living domestic cat in the world lived to be 38 years old. Créme Puff lived in Austin, Texas, and died in 2005. The average lifespan of an indoor cat is 15 years.

With good care, it is common for Birmans to live 15 years or more.

Exotic

With a flat face, snub nose, and short fur, Exotics are easy cats to spot. Their appearance has led to the nickname "teddy bear" cats. The nickname fits in well with their personalities too. Exotics are friendly, affectionate cats. They like to be around people. Exotics make great family pets and are known for their cleanliness. They are also good for families with busy lifestyles. Although they enjoy companionship, they are known to be independent cats sometimes. If they do want attention, they won't be shy. They may climb into your lap while you're reading or follow you from room to room.

In 2016, for the third year in a row, Exotics were ranked the most popular cat breed by the CFA, beating out their longhaired cousins such as the Persian and the Maine Coon.

FUN FACT: In 2014 the Exotic became the CFA's number one cat breed. It took over the top spot from the Persian, which had held it since the 1970s.

With their sweet expression and teddy-bear look, Exotics
are consistently one of the most popular cat breeds.

Exotic History

American Shorthair breeders developed the Exotic cat in the 1960s. Some breeders wanted their cats to have silver coats. Because some Persians had silver coats, breeders began crossing American Shorthairs with Persians.

Some of the resulting kittens had the desired silver coats. But they did not look like American Shorthairs. The kittens had short, plush coats, and their faces looked like those of Persians. Breeders became interested in these unique-looking cats with short coats. They began to cross Persians with other shorthaired cats such as Russian Blues and Burmese.

In 1966 the CFA accepted the new mixed breed as a separate breed. This breed was called the Exotic Shorthair. Later the name was changed to Exotic.

FUN FACT: Sterling was another name considered for the Exotic breed because of the silver hair of the first cats.

Exotics have a similar appearance to Persians
but the coat length of American Shorthairs.

Over the next 20 years, the CFA's Exotic breed standard changed often. In 1987 breeders decided that Exotics could only be crossbred with Persians.

Three years later, breeders came up with a simple way to describe the Exotic breed standard. Because an Exotic looks like a Persian cat, breeders thought the two breeds should have similar standards. Breeders decided that any future change made to the Persian standard would be made for the Exotic standard as well.

Modern Appearance

Because of the breed standard changes, today's Exotic cats look more like Persians than Exotics of the past. The only difference between Exotics and Persians is the length of the Exotic's coat. Modern breeders develop Exotics by crossing Persians with shorthaired cats. But breeders do this only once. The breeders then take the kittens from these matches and breed them with Persians. That's why modern Exotic kittens are almost entirely Persian.

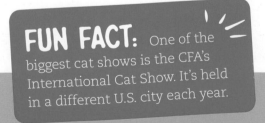

FUN FACT: One of the biggest cat shows is the CFA's International Cat Show. It's held in a different U.S. city each year.

Exotics are very similar to Persians (like the one pictured here) in both appearance and personality.

FUN FACT: Some people think that an Exotic's facial features give it a sad expression. Other people say that the mouth looks like a smile.

Exotic Traits

Exotics are medium-sized cats. Adult Exotics weigh between 8 and 15 pounds (3.6 and 6.8 kg). Their bodies are stocky and low to the ground. They have short, sturdy legs. Their paws are large and round, and their tails are short and thick.

Some Exotic kittens have long hair.

Coats

Exotics have short, plush coats made up of thick, soft fur. The fur does not tangle or **mat** as easily as the fur of a Persian cat. Exotics have a double coat. Thick, soft hair lies close to the skin. The thick layer of fur is covered by lighter, coarse fur.

Exotic cats have short hair because of their genes. Genes determine a cat's coat type, color, and gender. Kittens receive a pair of genes for each trait. They receive one gene from their mother and one gene from their father.

The gene for a shorthaired coat is dominant. Dominant genes are stronger than other genes. Cats with short coats need only one gene for short hair.

These genes can make it difficult to breed Exotic cats. Exotic kittens sometimes **inherit** one gene for long hair from each parent. These kittens will have long hair. They will look like Persians, but they are still considered to be Exotics. Some breed organizations recognize these cats as a different breed, the Exotic Longhair.

Some Exotics have solid white coats.

Facial Features

Exotics have unique faces that are only shared with Persian cats. Both breeds have snub noses and flat faces. But the fur on an Exotic's face is much shorter than the fur on a Persian's face.

Colors

Exotics can be many colors. The most common Exotic colors are black, tortoiseshell, red tabby, brown tabby, and bi-color. Tortoiseshell Exotics are covered in patches of red, black, and cream fur. Tabby Exotics' coats are mixed with dark, striped markings. Bi-color Exotics have coats with patches of white and another color. These colors include black, cream, red, tabby, or blue. Blue Exotics have blue-gray coats.

Personality

Exotics make excellent pets. They are known for their friendly and easygoing personalities. They get along well with dogs, children, and other cats. Exotics are playful but gentle cats. They like attention and often follow their owners around their homes. Some breeders say male Exotics tend to be more affectionate than females.

Exotics like to play with toys they can chew on or chase.

FUN FACT: Cats have an excellent sense of balance. They use their tails to walk on narrow paths without falling.

Caring for an Exotic

Grooming

Most cats do a good job of grooming their fur with their tongues. But sometimes an Exotic needs help from its owner. Their coat grows very thick in the winter. In late spring, Exotics begin to lose this thick coat. In spring and summer, Exotics should be combed more often than they are in the winter and fall.

You should comb your Exotic with a fine-toothed metal comb each week. Be gentle as you comb.

If your cat's fur does mat, you should never use scissors to cut out the mats. You could damage the coat or cut your cat's skin. Instead, have a professional groomer remove mats.

Exotics sometimes develop dark stains around their eyes. Tears easily leak out of Exotics' large eyes and down their flat faces. These tears contain **bacteria** that can stain Exotics' fur. You should clean around your cat's eyes every day with a moistened tissue or cloth.

Health Care

Exotics are strong, healthy cats. They can live 15 years or more with good care. Like other cats, Exotics should be kept indoors.

FUN FACT: Cats' tongues help them remove dirt and dead fur. They also help them spread natural oils, called **sebum**, through their fur.

You can use a cotton swab to gently clean around your Exotic's eyes.

Is an Exotic Right for You?

Exotics have a good balance in their personalities. They are affectionate and fun-loving, but they like to be alone sometimes. These traits make Exotics the perfect choice for families who are away from the house often. Exotics are also a popular breed because they have short hair and don't shed as much as some other cats.

People who are interested in owning an Exotic cat can look for one in several ways. They may contact animal shelters, breed rescue organizations, or breeders. Animal shelters or rescue organizations can be less expensive places to purchase an Exotic cat. Some rescue organizations specialize in finding homes for Exotics. The cats are usually adults and may even be registered.

Exotics from breeders can cost several hundred dollars. An added benefit of buying an Exotic from a breeder is that breeders often know the cat's parents and medical history. If you don't buy your cat from a breeder, be sure to ask about the cat's medical history.

FUN FACT: At least 74 million pet cats live in the United States, compared to about 70 million dogs. Many pet owners prefer cats because they don't require as much space as many dog breeds. Cats also don't need to be taken outside for walks as frequently as dogs.

Maine Coon

The Maine Coon is the largest native cat breed in North America. To go along with their large size, Maine Coons have big personalities. Their friendly, playful nature makes it easy to see why they're so popular. The Maine Coon's easygoing personality has even earned it a nickname — the "Gentle Giant" of the cat world.

Maine Coons are also admired for their beauty. These cats have silky, long coats and a kind expression. In the 1860s, the classy appearance of Maine Coons made them popular in early U.S. cat shows.

In 2016 the Maine Coon was the fifth most popular breed according to the CFA.

FUN FACT: Maine Coons are known for making soft, high-pitched chirping noises.

The Maine Coon's long, silky fur gives it an elegant look.

Maine Coon History

The Maine Coon is one of the oldest cat breeds in North America. The breed's long history has to do with its development. Most cat breeds are the result of careful breeding. Cat breeders select cats with desirable traits or qualities. Breeders then mate male and female cats that have these traits. Breeders hope that the resulting kittens will have the preferred characteristics.

The Maine Coon is considered a natural breed. A natural breed develops without interference from people. Because people didn't breed the Maine Coon, no one is certain how the breed came about. Several legends exist about this breed's history.

Popular Legends

One common legend says the Maine Coon breed developed from wild cats mating with raccoons. This belief comes from Maine Coons' bushy tails and some Maine Coons' brown tabby coloring. But this story is false. It is impossible for cats to breed with raccoons.

Another legend says that Maine Coons descended from royal cats in France. In the 1790s, France was at war. Marie Antoinette was France's queen. She wanted to escape to North America during the war. The queen asked Samuel Clough, a ship captain, to bring some of her valuable possessions to North America. She planned to follow a short time later.

Clough brought the queen's furniture, china, and six of her longhaired cats with him to Maine. But the queen never made it to Maine to claim her cats and possessions. She was killed during the war. Clough decided to keep the queen's cats in North America. According to the legend, these cats mated with native cats in North America, producing Maine Coons.

FUN FACT: One legend says that Vikings brought relatives of the Maine Coon to North America. The Vikings traveled to North America from Europe in the late 900s.

The brown tabby color pattern is very common in the Maine Coon breed.

The Real Story

Today most people agree that Maine Coon cats first came to North America from foreign countries. Long ago, many foreign ships traveled to the northeastern coast of North America to trade. Ship captains often brought cats along on these voyages to kill rats and mice on the ships.

These cats developed features that helped them handle difficult conditions onboard. They had large, sturdy frames. They also developed long coats that kept them warm and dry in cold, wet weather.

Ship cats often wandered ashore in search of food when ships stopped in North America. Many of these cats stayed in North America when the ships sailed home. These foreign cats mated with shorthaired cats native to North America. This breeding produced Maine Coons.

Gaining Popularity

During the late 1800s, Maine Coons were popular at cat shows in Maine, Massachusetts, and New York. In 1895 a Maine Coon received the Best Cat award at the famous Madison Square Garden show in New York City.

After the 1970s, Maine Coons made a huge comeback as show cats.

After 1895 Persian cats began to arrive in North America from Europe. More people wanted to own and breed Persians than Maine Coons. This change caused the number of Maine Coons in North America to decline.

But some breeders still admired Maine Coons. They worked hard to keep the breed alive. In 1975 the CFA recognized the Maine Coon as an official breed. By 1976 all North American cat registries recognized the breed. Over the next several years, Maine Coons won grand championship titles and other important awards at CFA shows.

FUN FACT: The Maine Coon received the first part of its name from the state of Maine. The breed is said to be native to the state. The second part of its name comes from the legend about raccoons.

Maine Coon Traits

Today most Maine Coons are household pets, and they no longer need to live on their own. But people still admire the unique features the Maine Coon naturally developed. From its large size to its square jaws, a Maine Coon has a look all its own.

Maine Coons can weigh as much as 20 pounds (9.1 kg). Male Maine Coons usually weigh between 13 and 18 pounds (5.9 and 8.2 kg). Females are slightly smaller. Most weigh between 8 and 12 pounds (3.6 and 5.4 kg).

Body

Maine Coons have sturdy, rectangular bodies that have good **proportion**. Muscular legs and large feet support the cat's solid frame. The breed's large paws are also thought to be an adaptation for Maine Coons to walk on top of snow, much like humans walk atop snow with snowshoes.

Maine Coons mature more slowly than most cat breeds. Maine Coons usually do not reach their full size until they are 3 to 5 years old. Most other cat breeds are fully grown at 1 year.

FUN FACT: Some cats have more than five claws or extra toes. These cats are known as polydactyls. Maine Coons with extra toes are not allowed to be shown at CFA shows.

FUN FACT: A Maine Coon's large feet help it walk over snow without sinking.

The Maine Coon's tail is often as long as its body.

Coats

Maine Coons have long, thick, fluffy coats. The fur on their legs and undersides is especially long to protect their bodies from the cold of ice and snow cover. The fur is shorter on their heads, shoulders, and backs to protect their bodies from getting caught on low-hanging branches and brush. A Maine Coon's coat is silky to the touch.

The length of Maine Coons' coats varies with the seasons. In winter their fur becomes thick and heavy. Winter coats can be 2 to 3 inches (5.1 to 7.6 centimeters) long. The breed's coat evolved to be water-repellant to help Maine Coons survive brutal Northern winters. Maine Coons shed their longer fur during the spring and summer.

Maine Coons often have a ruff, a fringe or frill of long hairs, around their necks. They also have tufts of fur on the tips of their ears and between their toes.

Ear tufts are common among longhaired breeds such as Maine Coons.

Tail

A Maine Coon's long, bushy tail is usually one of the first features people notice. The tail is wide at the base and tapers to a narrower point.

Facial Features

Maine Coons have square jaws with high cheekbones. Their oval-shaped eyes are large and set wide apart. Eye color varies. Their eyes can be either one color or a mixture of colors. Green, gold, and copper eyes are common.

FUN FACT: Maine Coons may wrap themselves in their bushy tails to keep warm.

Colors

Maine Coons can have almost any coat color. These colors include black, blue, red, cream, silver, and brown.

Maine Coons can also have one of many patterns. Many are solid or tabby. Others have a dark color with patches of white. Calico Maine Coons are white with patches of red and black.

The CFA does not register Maine Coons with colors that don't occur naturally. These include the colorpoint markings found in Siamese and Himalayan cats. Cats with colorpoints have light-colored coats with darker fur on their ears, feet, face, and tail.

Personality

Maine Coons are curious and playful. They want to be involved in the activities going on around them. Adult Maine Coons often run and play as kittens do. The cats' playfulness is a great source of entertainment for their owners.

Maine Coons are also loyal and friendly. These traits have led some people to call them the "dogs of the cat world." Like dogs, Maine Coons seem to enjoy attention from their owners. These cats can often be found sitting near their owners or following them around their homes.

FUN FACT: Cats mark territory with scent by rubbing against items with their cheeks and **flanks**. Cats have scent glands in these areas. The scent stays on the object and tells the other cats to stay away. Cats mark humans the same way.

Like other tabbies, red tabby Maine Coons have a
marking that looks like an "M" on their foreheads.

FUN FACT: In 2005 researchers discovered exactly how SMA is inherited. Owners can now test their cats for the disease before breeding them.

Caring for a Maine Coon

Grooming

Like other longhaired breeds, Maine Coons need regular brushing. Owners should brush Maine Coons once each week. Pure bristle brushes work best on Maine Coons. Combs work well on the thicker areas of the coat.

Maine Coons are sturdy, strong cats. With good care, they can live 12 to 15 years.

Exercise

Maine Coons are playful cats. A variety of toys will help keep your Maine Coon from becoming bored. Many cats enjoy chasing small balls or playing with toy mice.

Health Care

Maine Coons are generally very healthy, but they may develop some health problems. Some Maine Coons suffer from hip dysplasia. Cats with this condition have hip bones that do not fit together properly. Hip dysplasia makes movement difficult.

Maine Coons are also prone to the inherited diseases **cardiomyopathy** and spinal muscular atrophy (SMA). Cardiomyopathy is a serious heart disease that causes the heart walls to thicken or stretch. SMA causes muscle weakness and can affect movement.

Is a Maine Coon Right for You?

Maine Coons' playful, friendly personalities give their owners unexpected reasons to smile day after day. Though they've been said to have been mistaken as wild bobcats due to their large size, these good-natured cats make wonderful pets, even for large families. They seem to enjoy being around children, dogs, and other cats.

If you value plenty of playful interaction with your cat, a Maine Coon might be the right choice for you. Many Maine Coons are able to be trained to walk on leashes and to play fetch.

In general, they seem to enjoy being involved in their owners' activities. If you're reading a magazine or doing a crossword puzzle, you can expect your Maine Coon to be beside you.

If the Maine Coon is the right cat for you, the best place to buy a kitten is from a breeder. Most breeders take steps to be sure the kittens are healthy. Adoption from breed rescue groups and animal shelters is another way to find a Maine Coon.

FUN FACT: Cats are famous for their love of milk. However, many cats are lactose intolerant and shouldn't be given milk. These cats have trouble digesting the sugar, or lactose, in milk. It can cause an upset stomach.

Manx

No tail? No problem! The Manx is well known for being a tailless breed. In reality, the tails of Manx can be one of several types, from a full-grown tail to no tail at all. Manx with tails are sometimes mistaken as cats from another breed, but people can easily identify a tailless Manx.

The Manx is a medium-sized breed that can be longhaired or shorthaired. Its double coat makes it look bigger than it actually is. If the Manx doesn't have a tail, the back end has an oval shape. Add in a circular face and a broad head, and it's easy to see why the Manx is called the "rounded" cat.

The Manx is a popular breed in the CFA. The CFA considers shorthaired and longhaired Manx as the same breed. But other cat registries consider longhaired Manx a separate breed called the Cymric. The longhaired Manx has patches of longer hair on its neck and abdomen.

FUN FACT: The cat of any breed judged to be the very best cat in the competition receives the award of Best in Show.

Manx are well known for having round bodies and no tails.

Manx History

The Manx developed on the Isle of Man, an island between Great Britain and Ireland. It is the only cat bred specifically to have no tail. There are several legends that have tried to explain the origin of tailless cats.

One Manx legend involves the story of Noah's ark from the Bible. Noah was saving two of every animal from a great flood. The Manx was late getting onto the ark, and Noah was in a hurry to sail away. As the Manx came through the door, Noah accidentally slammed the ark's door on the cat's tail, cutting it off. All Manx from then on had no tails.

Another legend describes Viking warriors who invaded the Isle of Man in the 800s. These warriors decorated their helmets with animal tails. To keep their kittens safe, female Manx bit off their kittens' tails so the Vikings wouldn't kill them.

Yet another legend goes back to 1588, when ships from Spain attacked England. Some people think that tailless cats swam to the Isle of Man from one of the Spanish ships. However there are no records of tailless cats in Spain.

FUN FACT: Some people used to believe that a Manx was a cross between a cat and a rabbit. The people argued that some Manx hop like rabbits when they run. But a cat and a rabbit cannot mate and produce offspring.

The Manx is one of the oldest cat breeds in Europe.

Manx kittens inherit the tailless gene from their parents.

Heredity and Genetics

Although Manx legends are entertaining, they are not true. The real story most likely involves genes. Most people think that a genetic **mutation** caused Manx to be born without tails. A genetic mutation causes part of an animal's body to develop in a different way than normal. The mutation can be passed down to the animal's offspring.

Animals that lived on the Isle of Man had little contact with animals from other parts of the world. Therefore the tailless mutation was able to spread throughout the entire cat population. More and more cats inherited the mutation and were born without tails.

A shorthaired Manx named Cali won an award at a cat show at Madison Square Garden in New York City.

Gaining Popularity

Records of Manx on the Isle of Man begin about 300 years ago. In 1810 British painter Joseph Turner wrote that he had seven Manx that came from the Isle of Man.

People first displayed Manx in European cat shows in the 1870s. Many of the show cats had an uneven, hopping walk because their back legs were longer than their front legs. Today breeders try to breed cats that walk normally.

A shorthaired Manx first competed at a U.S. cat show in 1899. In 1958 a Manx named Mrs. Kelly of An-Si became the first Manx to win a CFA Grand Champion title. Longhaired Manx were not allowed to participate in cat shows until 1989. Today both longhaired and shorthaired Manx are popular show cats.

FUN FACT: The CFA officially recognized the Manx breed around 1920.

Manx Traits

Today's Manx look very much like the Manx of 300 years ago. These round, powerful cats often live long, healthy lives.

The Manx is a medium-sized cat. Most males weigh between 10 and 13 pounds (4.5 and 5.9 kg). Females are a little smaller, weighing between 7 and 11 pounds (3.2 and 5 kg).

Body

Manx have round heads and puffy cheeks. Regardless of whether they are shorthaired or longhaired, all Manx have a double coat of fur. The undercoat is dense and soft, while the outer coat is glossy and smooth.

The back legs of a Manx are longer than its front legs. The longer back legs make the back end stick up higher than the head. The cat's back curves up toward its muscular hind legs. Manx have an incredible jumping ability because of their powerful back legs. These cats are also fast runners and can quickly change directions.

FUN FACT: Manx have been called "race car cats" because of their speed and ability to make sharp turns.

Cat trees are perfect for Manx. The cats can jump to one of the platforms and **perch** high off the ground.

Rumpies have a small indent at the end
of their spine where a tail would be.

Tail Types

A Manx is often described by its tail type. A Manx can have a long tail, a stumpy tail, a riser tail, or no tail. The cats are nicknamed by the type of tail they have. Manx with full tails are called longies, while cats with short, stumpy tails are called stumpies. Manx with no tails are called rumpies.

The last type of Manx are known as risers. These cats have a small bump of **cartilage** where the tail normally starts. Rumpies and risers are the only types of Manx that can compete at cat shows.

Coats

Manx cats can be longhaired or shorthaired, though shorthaired Manx are more common. Longhaired Manx are also known as Cymric. They are thought to have been crossbred with longhaired breeds such as the Himalayan or Persian.

Some cat registries recognize the Cymric as a separate breed, but the CFA considers the Cymric to be a variety of the Manx breed. Both longhaired and shorthaired Manx have double-layered coats.

Manx with a bump at the end of their spine are also called rumpy-risers.

FUN FACT: All four tail types can occur in kittens from the same litter.

This Manx cat has a calico coat, made up
of a mixture of black, red, and white hairs.

Colors

The fur of a Manx comes in almost every color and pattern. Common colors are white, black, cream, silver, blue, and red. Tabby, calico, and tortoiseshell coats also are common. Calico cats are white with black and red patches. The coats of tortoiseshell cats may have a few white markings but are mostly black and red.

Manx cats are people-oriented. They like to be around their human families as much as possible.

Personality

Manx are known as a playful breed. They seem to prefer toys that allow them to be active. On top of being athletic, Manx are also smart. Some Manx can learn commands and how to open doors.

Manx are social cats. They get along well with children and enjoy being around other cats and dogs. These cats are loyal and often seek attention. Many Manx become very close to their owners.

FUN FACT: Ever find your cat sleeping on a pile of unwashed laundry? Cats find their owner's scent comforting, just like their mother's scent was comforting to them as kittens.

Caring for a Manx

Health Care

Manx are considered to be a healthy breed and can live 15 years or more with proper care. Manx longies and stumpies can develop problems such as **arthritis** in their tails. To avoid this problem, breeders may cut off the cat's tail at birth.

Grooming

Shorthaired Manx need little grooming and only need to be brushed once a week. Longhaired Manx should be brushed daily. Use a soft bristle brush to remove any loose hair. After you finish brushing, use a comb to smooth out the cat's fur. Good grooming can help keep your Manx from developing hairballs.

Is a Manx Right for You?

If you're looking for a quiet but playful pet, a Manx could be right for you. The cat's powerful back legs make it a natural jumper and a fast runner. Manx love to leap for toys or chase them around the room. The Manx is also known to have doglike habits, such as fetching an item for its owner or burying its toys. These cats also have the loyalty of a dog and become closely attached to their owners.

If you are interested in making a Manx your pet, you have several options. If you want a purebred Manx, you should visit a breeder. Most breeders register their cats and kittens. Registered cats have papers that list the names of the breeder, the cat's parents, and sometimes the cat's other relatives. You can also contact an animal shelter or rescue organization to adopt a Manx.

FUN FACT: You should always provide your cat plenty of water. A dehydrated cat can have problems with circulation, digestion, and removing waste from its body.

A Longhaired Manx

Ocicat

When seeing an Ocicat for the first time, some people wonder if it is tame or wild. The Ocicat's spotted coat makes it look like a wildcat. But the Ocicat does not have a wild personality. It is a friendly cat that is as tame as members of other domestic cat breeds.

Much of the Ocicat's popularity has to do with its appearance. The Ocicat is the only spotted domestic breed developed specifically to look like a wildcat. Like Abyssinians, Ocicats also have agouti coats, which adds to their unique look.

FUN FACT: Most cats dislike water. But many Ocicats seem to enjoy playing in it.

The Ocicat's unique spotted coat pattern
attracts many people to the breed.

An Ocelot

Ocicat History

Compared to other cat breeds, the Ocicat is fairly new. The first Ocicats were bred about 50 years ago. Ocicats are mostly Siamese, but they are also part Abyssinian.

The ocelot and the Ocicat have similar spotted patterns.

Tonga

In 1964 a Michigan cat breeder named Virginia Daly was working toward a goal. She was trying to produce a Siamese cat with colorpoints that looked like an Abyssinian's agouti coat.

Daly first bred an Abyssinian and a Siamese cat. She named a female kitten from this mating Dalai She. Daly then bred Dalai She to a Siamese named Whitehead Elegante Sun. When Daly mated these two cats again, she got a surprise. One kitten from this mating didn't look like the other cats the matings had produced. This kitten had ivory fur and bright golden spots. Daly named the cat Tonga. Daly's daughter called him an "ocicat" because Tonga looked like a wildcat called the ocelot. Daly had Tonga neutered so he could not **reproduce**. She then sold him as a pet.

FUN FACT: In 1965 Tonga was entered in a CFA cat show in the special exhibit category. The catalog said the breeds in this category were "breeds of the future."

A New Breed Takes Off

Daly later wrote to Dr. Clyde Keeler of Georgia University. Keeler was interested in creating a cat that looked like the Egyptian Spotted Fishing Cat. This extinct cat lived in ancient Egypt.

Daly told Keeler that she had produced a spotted cat. Keeler encouraged Daly to try to make a new cat breed by producing more spotted kittens.

Daly bred Tonga's parents again. They produced what Daly had hoped for — another spotted kitten. Daly named this kitten Dalai Dotson. Dalai Dotson and other spotted kittens like him soon became known as Ocicats.

Other breeders began working with Ocicats. They bred some Ocicats with American Shorthairs.

Breeding with American Shorthairs, like the cat above, gave Ocicats larger, stronger bodies.

FUN FACT: In 1970 the town that Virginia Daly lived in passed a law that delayed her breeding efforts. The law limited the number of cats people could own.

Ocicat Moirai Wedjat won the "Best of the Best" prize at a CFA show at Madison Square Garden in New York City.

Ocicats began appearing at cat shows in the late 1960s. The International Cat Association (TICA) officially recognized the breed in 1986. In 1987 the CFA recognized the Ocicat.

Gaining Popularity

After the CFA recognized the Ocicat, the breed quickly gained popularity. By 1988 the Ocicat was the 14th most popular breed out of 35 CFA breeds.

The Ocicat also quickly earned awards at CFA shows. In September 1987, an Ocicat was named a Grand Champion for the first time. In the 1991–1992 show season, an Ocicat received a National Winner title for the first time.

Since then, Ocicats have won many important CFA titles and awards, including an award at the national show for Best Kitten in 2013–2014. The Kitten of the Year award for this show went to a beautiful chocolate spotted Ocicat named "GC, NW DotDotDot BornintheUSA of Wild Rain." He is nicknamed Uncle Sam.

FUN FACT: In the early 1990s, Ocicats were separated into color classes for CFA shows. Before this time, Ocicats of all colors competed in the same class.

Ocicat Traits

Ocicats are medium in size. Males usually weigh 11 to 14 pounds (5 to 6.4 kg). Females are smaller. They usually weigh between 6 and 10 pounds (2.7 and 4.5 kg).

Body

The Ocicat's body is solid and muscular. Long, strong legs help support its frame. The shoulders and chest are deep and broad. The back is level or slightly higher in the rear.

Although the Ocicat is strong, it isn't bulky. Instead, the Ocicat has the sleek, graceful appearance of a well-trained athlete. The cat's dense bones and muscles make it heavier than it looks.

An Ocicat's short, smooth fur lies close to its body. The coat is glossy and feels soft like satin.

Patterns and Colors

The Ocicat's agouti coat has a dark spotted pattern on a lighter background color. Background coat colors include tawny, ivory, honey, blue, and silver. Tawny is a ticked brown color. Blue is a blue-gray color, and silver is almost white.

An Ocicat's thumb-shaped spots can be black, chocolate, cinnamon, fawn, blue, or lavender. Fawn is a light shade of the red-brown cinnamon color. Lavender is a lighter shade of chocolate that has a pink tint. An Ocicat's spots are always darker than the rest of the fur. At cat shows, judges prefer well-defined spots instead of faint ones.

FUN FACT: Sometimes breeders have difficulty deciding the color of an Ocicat. In these cases, they use the tail tip to identify the correct color.

Ocicats can have one of several background colors, including silver (left) and tawny (right).

Ocicats have M-shaped markings on their foreheads.

The CFA accepts Ocicats in 12 color patterns. These patterns come from combinations of background and spot colors. Six of the colors are based off the silver background. They are ebony silver, chocolate silver, cinnamon silver, blue silver, lavender silver, and fawn silver.

The other six color patterns have varying backgrounds according to the spot color. These patterns are tawny, chocolate, cinnamon, blue, lavender, and fawn.

Leaving toys out for your Ocicat will help keep it active while you are away.

Some Ocicats do not meet the breed standard. These cats may have one solid color or have tabby stripes rather than spots. Ocicats without spots cannot compete in CFA cat shows.

Facial Features

Like the Siamese cat, the Ocicat has a wedge-shaped head. Its ears are alert and wide. The ears may have pointed tufts of hair at the tips. The Ocicat's large, almond-shaped eyes angle toward the ears.

Personality

Many people say the Ocicat's personality is more like a dog than a cat. Ocicats seem to enjoy spending time with their owners. The cats often follow their owners around. Some Ocicats will ride on their owners' shoulders.

Ocicats are smart. They sometimes can be trained to do tricks and walk on a leash. Some owners teach their Ocicats to fetch.

Ocicats are an active breed. But they are less active than some of their shorthaired cousins such as the Oriental. The Ocicat's athletic build helps it jump high and run quickly.

FUN FACT: Many owners bring their Ocicats with them when they travel. The cats easily adjust to new surroundings.

An Ocicat that has another cat to play with is less likely to become bored when its owners are away.

Caring for an Ocicat

Health Care

The Ocicat is a very healthy breed. Ocicats can live 15 to 20 years with proper care.

Grooming

An Ocicat's short coat needs little grooming. Ocicats should be brushed with a soft bristle or rubber brush weekly.

After brushing, you should use a coarse comb to smooth out your cat's fur. Some owners rub their Ocicats with a soft cloth called a chamois, which helps keep their coats shiny.

Is an Ocicat Right for You?

Ocicats make great family pets for many households. Ocicats are healthy and need little special care. These friendly, curious cats seem to like being around people. They enjoy the company of both cats and dogs. If you're away from home often, it's best to have a companion animal for your Ocicat.

You can find an Ocicat in several ways. Many people buy Ocicats from breeders. Breeders often charge several hundred dollars for an Ocicat. Other people adopt Ocicats from rescue organizations.

Occasionally, people can adopt Ocicats from animal shelters. But most shelters have mixed-breed cats instead of purebred cats such as the Ocicat.

FUN FACT: Ocicats are a vocal breed, but they don't have the raspy yowl of their Siamese relatives.

Oriental

The Oriental cat reminds many people of its close relative, the Siamese. The Oriental and the Siamese share wedge-shaped heads, large ears, and slim bodies. But Orientals can claim one feature all to themselves — color! All Siamese cats have colorpoints. But Orientals' coats can be one of more than 300 colors or color patterns.

The personality of Orientals is just as colorful as their coats. These cats are curious, playful, and loyal. They often want to be involved in their owners' activities. Orientals will quickly investigate the contents of an open drawer, purse, or backpack.

The Oriental's sleek look and energetic personality help make it a popular cat.

FUN FACT: Orientals' many colors have led some people to nickname them "Ornamentals."

Many Orientals' coats have a mixture of two or more colors.

Oriental History

The Oriental Shorthair breed began in Great Britain about 50 years ago. The Oriental Longhair breed developed about 30 years later in Great Britain and the United States. Both types developed through careful breeding.

The First Orientals

The first Orientals were bred in Great Britain during the 1950s. Breeders wanted a cat that had a long, narrow body like the Siamese cat. But they wanted the cat to have different colors and patterns from the Siamese.

People bred Siamese cats to Persians, Korats, British Shorthairs, Russian Blues, and Abyssinians. These matings led to a large variety of colors and patterns.

In Great Britain, the resulting cats had several names at first. Brown solid-colored cats were called Havanas. Cats with solid-colored fur of another color were called Foreigns. But by the 1970s, the cats were all known as Oriental Shorthairs.

FUN FACT: Like Siamese cats, most Orientals have loud meows.

Orientals have wedge-shaped heads and large ears much like their Siamese relatives.

Oriental Shorthairs that compete in shows are expertly groomed, with shiny coats and clean ears.

FUN FACT: The first Oriental Shorthair to win the CFA breed winner title was a tabby female named Sand 'N' Sea Bikkuri of Jemwyck.

In 1972 U.S. cat breeders Peter and Vicky Markstein visited Great Britain and saw Oriental Shorthairs. The Marksteins helped bring several Oriental Shorthairs to the United States. These cats began the Oriental Shorthair breed in North America. In 1977 the CFA accepted the Oriental Shorthair for championship status, allowing it to compete for top awards. The Oriental Shorthair soon became one of the CFA's most popular breeds.

Oriental Longhairs have medium-length coats that lie close to their bodies.

Oriental Longhairs Appear

In the 1980s, several breeders in Great Britain and the United States began trying to breed longhaired Orientals. These breeders mated Oriental Shorthairs with longhaired cat breeds such as the Balinese. The resulting kittens looked like Oriental Shorthairs, but they had longer, silkier fur.

Today Oriental Longhairs compete in most cat shows. In 1985 TICA accepted Oriental Longhairs for competition. The CFA accepted the breed in 1995. In 1996 the CFA combined the Oriental Longhair and the Oriental Shorthair into one breed division called the Oriental.

FUN FACT: Most longhaired cats have double coats. But the Oriental Longhair has only one layer of fur.

The slim body of the Oriental gives it a graceful look.

Oriental Traits

Greyhound Dog

Orientals are small-sized cats. Male Orientals usually weigh 7 to 11 pounds (3.2 to 5 kg). Females are smaller. They usually weigh 5 to 9 pounds (2.3 to 4 kg).

Body

The Oriental's body is shaped like a tube. People sometimes compare Orientals to Greyhound dogs. Like the Greyhound, the Oriental has a long, narrow body. The Oriental Shorthair's long, thin tail also looks like the tail of a Greyhound dog.

Orientals have narrow shoulders and long, slim legs. The back legs are a little longer than the front legs.

The Oriental's slender body might lead people to believe that the cat is weak. But the Oriental is a muscular cat that is stronger than it appears.

Coat

An Oriental's fur lies close to its body. An Oriental Shorthair's fur is fine and smooth. Oriental Longhairs have medium-length fur. It is softer and silkier than the fur of Oriental Shorthairs. An Oriental Longhair's tail spreads out like a long, fluffy feather.

FUN FACT: Orientals' long, slender back legs allow the cats to climb and jump easily.

Colors

Orientals' coats have a great variety of colors and color patterns. Common solid colors are black, white, chestnut, cinnamon, blue, red, and lavender. Chestnut and cinnamon are shades of brown. Blue is a shade of gray, and lavender is pink-gray.

Shaded Orientals have white undercoats. Certain parts of the body have colored tips at the end of each hair. The tipping can be lavender, cinnamon, or other colors. It often appears on a cat's sides, face, and tail.

Smoke Orientals appear to be one solid color. But each hair on a smoke Oriental has a narrow band of white at the base.

Other color patterns include tabby and tortoiseshell. Tabby Orientals have striped, swirled, spotted, or ticked markings. Tortoiseshell Orientals have black, brown, or cinnamon coats that are mixed with patches of red-orange hair.

Some Orientals have colorpoints like Siamese cats do. The points range in color. The seal-point Oriental has very dark brown points. Lilac-point Orientals have frosty gray points that have a slight pink tone.

Oriental kittens from the same litter often have a wide variety of color patterns.

FUN FACT: Orientals lead the pack when it comes to variety. Their coats come in the most color and pattern combinations, beating out all other cat breeds.

Orientals' eyes are almond-shaped and slanted toward the nose.

Facial Features

An Oriental's wedge-shaped head looks like an upside-down triangle. The nose is long and straight. The ears are large, wide, and pointed. Nearly all Oriental cats have green eyes. But some Orientals have blue eyes. An Oriental also may have one blue eye and one green eye.

Personality

Orientals make good family pets. They usually get along well with children. They also do well in homes that have other cats or dogs.

Orientals seem to like being the center of attention. They often try to be involved in all of their owners' activities. Whether you're reading a book or watching TV, you can expect your Oriental to be nearby.

Orientals are playful cats. They may pick up and play with objects such as pens, gloves, and watches. Some cat breeds are playful only as kittens. But Orientals remain playful as adults.

FUN FACT: Like their Siamese relatives, Orientals are known for bonding closely with one person.

Caring for an Oriental

Health Care
Oriental cats have few health problems and can live 20 years or more when properly cared for.

Grooming
Oriental Shorthairs need little grooming. These cats only need to be brushed once each week with a soft bristle brush. For extra shine, you can wipe the cat's coat with your hands or a chamois.

Oriental Longhairs need more grooming. Owners should comb their Longhaired Orientals' fur each day with a metal comb.

Is an Oriental Right for You?
The Oriental is a friendly, playful breed. Many people enjoy the breed's active personality. However, these cats can demand a great deal of attention from their owners. Orientals do not seem to like being alone for long periods of time. If your family is gone for most of the day, your Oriental should have the company of another cat or a dog.

If you think the Oriental breed is right for your home, you can find one in several ways. Most people choose to buy Orientals from breeders. Breeders often sell retired show cats for less money than kittens would cost.

Some people adopt Orientals from breed rescue organizations. Occasionally people can adopt Orientals from animal shelters. But most shelters have mixed-breed cats instead of purebred cats such as the Oriental.

FUN FACT: Orientals are easy to train. Some people train their Orientals to fetch.

122

Oriental kittens often become closely
bonded with their human owners.

Persian

Persians are one of the best known and most popular cat breeds in the world. The Persian was the most popular breed in the CFA from 2005 to 2009. The breed also topped the CFA popularity list often before 2005. In 2016, the CFA ranked the Persian fourth among most popular cat breeds.

When you consider Persians' traits, it is easy to see why these cats top popularity lists. A Persian's long, silky coat is one of its most attractive features. Persians also have unique facial features. The face has a flat, pushed-in appearance. Many people think the Persian's face gives it a sweet expression.

FUN FACT: Many people say Persians communicate with their eyes instead of their voices.

A popular legend about the first-ever Persian describes a cat similar in appearance to today's smoke-colored Persians.

The Persian's short nose helps people recognize the breed.

Persian History

The Persian is one of the oldest cat breeds. Much of the Persian's history is unknown. The breed's mysterious background has led people to tell stories about how it came about.

A Magical Legend

One legend tells the story of a merchant who came across a group of robbers attacking a stranger. The merchant fought off the thieves and cared for the injured stranger.

After he recovered, the stranger told the merchant that he was a magician. He promised the merchant one wish in payment for saving his life. But the merchant did not want a wish. He was happy with his life. He told the magician that he liked to sit under the sparkling stars at night. He also said he liked to watch the smoke swirl from a crackling fire.

A Turkish Angora

The magician said that he could give the merchant the things he mentioned. The magician took a swirl of smoke, a spear of fire, and the light of two stars. The magician then created a cat with a fire-tipped tongue, smoke-gray fur, and sparkling eyes. The legend says that it was the first Persian cat.

The Real Story

Most people think the Persian descended from longhaired Asian cats. Manuscripts and drawings from as early as 1684 BC show cats that look like Persians.

In the 1500s, European sailors and merchants often traveled to the Asian regions of Turkey and Persia. Today Persia is the country of Iran. These sailors and merchants brought longhaired cats back to Europe. The Turkish cats were called Angoras. The cats from Persia were called Persians. Both of these longhaired cats soon became popular with European royal families.

FUN FACT: Other cat breeds have also been kept and valued by royalty. These breeds include the Birman and the Siamese.

FUN FACT: Today British people still call Persians longhairs or Persian longhairs.

Early Angoras and Persians looked alike. But differences between the two breeds developed by the late 1800s. Persians were heavier than Angoras. Their coats were thicker. Persians also had larger heads and rounder eyes than Angoras.

From Europe to North America

By 1903 Persians were recognized as a separate breed in Great Britain. But they were called longhairs instead of Persians.

A breeder shows off her prize-winning Persian in 1935.

After 1895 people brought Persians to North America from Europe. The Persian soon became very popular in shows and as pets.

In 1906 the CFA formed. A Persian named Molly Bond was one of the first cats registered. In 1914 the CFA formed a breed standard for Persians. This standard created color classes for Persians at shows. The standard was very similar to earlier British breed standards for Persians.

Changing Looks

Over time, cat breeders wanted the Persian to have a certain look. They carefully chose cats with specific traits that they wanted to continue in the breed. Because of this breeding, today's Persians look different than they once did. Modern Persians have shorter, more **compact** bodies than Persians of the early 1900s. Today's Persians also have thicker, longer fur than the original Persians did.

The biggest change in the Persian's appearance is in its face. Early Persians had wedge-shaped heads with long noses. But today's Persians have larger, more rounded heads. Their noses are also much shorter.

Persian Traits

Persian cats come in a wide range of sizes. Adults weigh 5 to 15 pounds (2.3 to 6.8 kg). Females are usually smaller than males.

Body

Persians have short, stocky bodies that appear well-balanced. The chest is broad and deep. Short, thick legs and large, round paws add to the Persian's sturdy look.

Coats

Of all the Persian's features, the coat attracts the most attention. Persians have double coats of long, soft fur. The fur is thick and plush near the skin. This thick layer of fur is covered by lighter, silky fur. The outer coat can be 6 to 8 inches (15 to 20 cm) long.

A Persian's coat is heavier during the winter. During spring and summer, Persians shed this heavier coat.

A Persian also has thick, flowing fur on its tail and a ruff around its neck. The ruff comes to a point between the front legs.

FUN FACT: A cat's whiskers help it gather information about its surroundings. They can measure distance, detect movement, and sense vibrations.

The Persian's long, heavy coat can add
to the cat's stocky appearance.

Solid Persian (left), Tabby Persian (right)

CFA Color Divisions

Persians can be one of many colors and color combinations. The CFA divides Persians into seven color divisions for competition. These divisions include solid, shaded and smoke, tabby, and calico and bi-color. Parti-color, silver and golden, and Himalayan make up the other three color divisions.

Solid, Shaded, and Smoked Persians

Solid-colored Persians have undercoats and overcoats of one solid color. These colors may be white, black, blue, red, cream, chocolate, or lilac. Blue is a shade of gray. Lilac Persians have pink-gray coats.

Shaded Persians have white coats with colored tips at the end of each hair. These tips can be red, cream, black, or blue. Some shaded Persians have two or more colors of tips.

Smoke Persians may appear to be one color. But they actually have a white undercoat with a darker overcoat.

A Rainbow of Colors

Many Persians have a mix of more than one color. Tabby Persians have coats with dark striped markings. Their coats can be silver, red, brown, blue, or other colors. Bi-color Persians have coats with patches of white and another solid color. Calico Persians are tri-colored cats with red, black, and white patches.

Parti-colored Persians' coats have patches of two or more colors. These color combinations include tortoiseshell, blue-cream, and lilac-cream. Tortoiseshell Persians have black or brown fur with red patches.

FUN FACT: Blue and silver Persians were especially popular with early Persian owners in the United States.

Seal-point Himalayans have very dark brown colorpoints.

Silver and Golden Persians

Silver Persians have white coats. But each hair has a black tip. This coloring makes the cat's coat appear silver. Golden Persians also have black-tipped coats, but their coats are cream instead of white. Silver and golden Persians have features not found in other Persian cats. These Persians' faces are less flat than those of other Persians. Silver and golden Persians also have thick black rims around their eyes.

Himalayan Persians

Himalayan Persians resulted from mating Persian and Siamese cats. These cats have the compact body, long fur, and flat face of other Persians. They have colorpoints and blue eyes like Siamese cats.

The CFA considers Himalayans to be part of the Persian breed. But some other registries consider Himalayans to be a separate breed.

Facial Features

Persians have large, round heads with full cheeks and broad jaws. Their large, rounded eyes are set wide apart. The Persian's short, snub nose makes its face look flat. The nose has a dent called a break between the eyes. A Persian's small, rounded ears tilt slightly forward.

Personality

Persians are known for their calm, gentle personalities. They are among the quietest and least active of all cat breeds.

Persians also are friendly and affectionate. They seem to enjoy sitting on humans' laps and being petted. They get along well with other animals.

FUN FACT: Many cats enjoy climbing and jumping on top of objects high above the ground. But Persians seem to prefer being on the ground.

Caring for a Persian

Health Care

Persians can have some health problems. Cats often swallow fur as they groom their coats with their tongues. Because Persians have long hair, they are more likely to get hairballs. If hairballs become too large, they can lodge in the cat's digestive system. A vet then may need to remove these hairballs. Regular combing is the best way to prevent hairballs.

Persians' short noses can cause breathing problems. These problems may lead to respiratory illnesses.

Persians can also develop a serious illness called polycystic kidney disease. This disease causes cats' kidneys to stop working properly. The disease is passed to kittens through their parents. Responsible breeders do tests for polycystic kidney disease before using cats for breeding.

Grooming

Persians' long coats must be groomed with a wide-toothed metal comb daily to prevent mats. If mats do occur, owners should not cut them out with scissors. Cutting out mats can injure your cat's skin or damage its coat. Instead, use a small-toothed comb to untangle mats or have a veterinarian take care of them.

Most cats do not need baths. But Persians' long coats should be bathed about once every three months. Owners should use a shampoo made for cats.

Persians' large eyes and flat faces allow tears to easily leak out of their eyes. Bacteria in tears can stain their fur. To prevent these stains, clean around your Persian's eyes daily with a moistened tissue, cotton swab, or cloth.

FUN FACT: With good care, Persians can live more than 15 years.

If your cat suddenly stops using its litter box, it could be a sign of illness such as a urinary tract infection or kidney or liver issues. Call your vet right away.

A dog can be a good companion for a Persian.

Is a Persian Right for You?

Persians can live comfortably in a variety of households. Their quiet personalities make them best suited for calm living environments. But they can adapt to living in very active households with children. Persians also get along well with dogs and other cats.

In general, Persians are healthy cats that are easy to care for. But the Persian's long coat does need daily grooming to keep it healthy and attractive.

If you decide the Persian is right for you, you can find one in several ways. Many people contact breeders or pet stores. Persians from these sources can cost several hundred dollars. However, breeders usually know the cat's history. Knowing the cat's history helps you be sure you are getting a healthy cat.

Breed rescue organizations and animal shelters can be less expensive places to get Persians. These organizations take care of pets until the animals can be placed in new homes. Rescue organizations may even have registered cats.

Shelters often have mixed-breed pets available instead of purebred animals such as the Persian. Many cat shows don't allow mixed-breed cats to compete. But a mixed-breed Persian can still make an excellent pet.

FUN FACT: Because of their calm personalities, Persians make great pets for apartment living.

Ragdoll

Many cats are named for their place of origin. Others are named for their physical characteristics. But the Ragdoll gets its name from a behavior. When picked up, some Ragdolls go limp, resembling a rag doll toy.

The Ragdoll breed has gained widespread popularity throughout the world. In 2016 the Ragdoll was the second most popular breed in the CFA.

Many people enjoy the unique combination of the Ragdoll's personality and appearance. Ragdolls make a big statement with their large size, colorpoints, and silky fur. Yet the cats have understated personalities. Ragdolls are quiet, gentle, and affectionate. The breed's personality makes it popular with people who want a calm companion.

FUN FACT: Ragdolls are similar in appearance and personality to Maine Coon cats. Both breeds have earned the nickname "gentle giants."

The long, thick coat of the Ragdoll adds
to its full-bodied appearance.

Ragdoll History

The Ragdoll is one of the newest cat breeds. It was developed in the 1960s in California.

A Popular Myth

A myth exists about the origin of Ragdolls. This story says that the breed was created after a car accidentally struck a pregnant longhaired white cat. The cat's brain was damaged as a result of the accident. This injury changed the cat's personality. The cat became extremely quiet and gentle. Following the accident, the cat's body also went limp when held. The cat later gave birth to kittens. These kittens were born with the same limp body and gentle personality as their mother.

This story about Ragdolls is not true. A cat's personality and physical condition can change as a result of an accident. But it is impossible for these changes to be passed to the cat's offspring.

FUN FACT: TV and social media star Grumpy Cat has markings similar to a Himalayan or Ragdoll, but her parents were a calico and a gray tabby. Grumpy Cat's real name is Tardar Sauce.

Ragdoll kittens often look and act similar to their parents.

Ann Baker holds Fugianna, a female cat
that helped develop the Ragdoll breed.

A New Breed Takes Off

Ann Baker of Riverside, California, developed the Ragdoll breed in the early 1960s. Baker bred a longhaired white cat named Josephine to another longhaired cat. It is believed that these cats had markings similar to those of the Siamese, a breed with colorpoints. The mating produced a **mitted**, seal-point male named Daddy Warbucks. This cat had a cream-colored coat with dark points. He also had white markings on all four of his paws.

Many people believe Daddy Warbucks and other relatives of Josephine are the breed's foundation cats. It is not known what breeds Baker used to develop the Ragdoll. Some people believe Baker used Persian, Birman, and Burmese cats. Other people don't believe Baker used purebred cats. They think she selected mixed-breed longhaired cats with certain features for her breeding program.

Daddy Warbucks (above) is known for developing the mitted color pattern in the Ragdoll breed.

FUN FACT: Purring is the sound of a mellow cat. Or is it? Scientists aren't sure. Cats purr when they are snuggled on a lap. Cats also purr when they are injured, sick, and anxious. A purr may be a way for a cat to comfort itself.

A New Breed is Recognized

In 1971 Baker founded the International Ragdoll Cat Association (IRCA). Baker had strict rules about how her Ragdolls should be bred. But cat associations did not recognize IRCA Ragdolls. Owners could not enter these cats in cat shows.

Other breeders did not agree with the IRCA rules. Two of these breeders were Denny and Laura Dayton. The Daytons decided to develop the breed so that other cat associations would accept it.

The Daytons bought a pair of IRCA Ragdolls. Starting with these two cats, they created a standard breeding program for Ragdolls. In 1975 the Daytons and other Ragdoll breeders formed the Ragdoll Fanciers Club International. This club tried to build interest in the breed.

Eventually, the breeders' work paid off. The CFA allowed the Ragdoll to be shown in its miscellaneous class in 1993. In 2000 the CFA officially accepted the Ragdoll.

FUN FACT: Ragdolls have quiet meows. They meow less than many other breeds.

Ragdoll Traits

Ragdolls are large cats. They can weigh 20 pounds (9.1 kg) or more. Male Ragdolls usually weigh between 14 and 18 pounds (6.4 and 8.2 kg). Females usually weigh between 8 and 12 pounds (3.6 and 5.4 kg). It may take up to four years for Ragdolls to reach their full size.

Body

Ragdolls have sturdy, long bodies with good proportion. Broad legs and large, round paws support the cats' muscular frames. Ragdolls have full, long tails.

Coat

A Ragdoll's fur is long, thick, and soft. Ragdolls have a double coat. A thin layer of plush fur lies near the skin. This undercoat is covered by a layer of lightweight, long, silky fur. The Ragdoll's fur does not easily clump together in mats like the coats of some other longhaired breeds.

Ragdolls often have a ruff. The hair on their faces and shoulders is often shorter than it is on the rest of their bodies.

FUN FACT: Ragdolls may have tufts of fur between their toes.

Some Ragdolls have dark brown colorpoints that stand out against their light body color.

Mitted Ragdoll

Point Colors

All Ragdolls have colorpoints. Ragdoll kittens are born white. The points begin to appear when the kittens are a few days old. Ragdolls' permanent coat color patterns develop by the time they are 4 years old.

Ragdolls that have no color pattern other than points are simply called colorpoints. A colorpoint Ragdoll's coat has no white fur.

Points can be one of several colors. These colors include seal, chocolate, blue, and lilac. Points can also be red, cinnamon, cream, and fawn. Seal is dark brown, and chocolate is light brown. The blue color is blue-gray, and the lilac color is pink-gray. Red-point Ragdolls have red-orange points. On cinnamon-point Ragdolls, the points are red-brown. Cream ranges from dark off-white to very light brown. The fawn color is light yellow-brown.

Point Color Patterns

Ragdolls may have solid points, lynx points, or tortie points. Ragdolls with lynx points have lightly striped coats and heavily striped points. Tortie-point Ragdolls have points with patches of black, red, and cream.

Other Color Patterns

Some Ragdolls are mitted. Like colorpoints, these cats have dark points and light-colored bodies. But a mitted Ragdoll has white mitts on its front paws. White "boots" are on its back legs and feet. A mitted Ragdoll also has a white stripe on its stomach, a white chin, and a white chest.

Van Ragdolls are mostly white. They have dark markings on their ears, tail, and the top area of their face. They also may have a couple of dark markings on their bodies.

Red-point Ragdoll

FUN FACT: The points and color patterns of a Ragdoll darken as the cat gets older.

Bi-color Ragdoll

FUN FACT: Each registry has different rules about which Ragdoll colors and patterns are allowed in cat shows.

Bi-color Ragdolls have dark points on their ears, tail, and the outer parts of their faces. All four legs, the underbody, and the chest are white. Bi-colors have white upside-down "V" markings on their faces. They also may have some white on their backs.

Ragdolls are calm as adults, but Ragdoll kittens are very playful.

Facial Features

A Ragdoll's head is wide and shaped like a wedge. This shape looks like an upside-down triangle. Its ears are wide at the base and rounded at the top. The ears also tip forward. All Ragdolls have blue, oval-shaped eyes.

Personality

Ragdolls are friendly cats. They seem to enjoy being around people and other animals. Although they don't crave constant attention, Ragdolls may follow people around. They seem to enjoy quietly watching the people and animals around them. Ragdolls also seem to enjoy being held.

Ragdolls are known for their intelligence. Many can be trained to play fetch or to follow other basic commands.

FUN FACT: Many cats seem to enjoy jumping onto tall objects. But Ragdolls often stay on the floor instead.

Caring for a Ragdoll

Health Care

Ragdoll cats have few health problems. The most common problem is hairballs. Regular brushing is the best way to prevent hairballs. Brushing removes loose fur before the cat can swallow it.

A myth about Ragdolls says the cats have bones or muscles that have not formed correctly. Some people believe that this physical **deformity** is the reason Ragdolls' bodies relax when held. But the breed does not have any physical deformities. No one knows why some Ragdoll cats relax their muscles when they are picked up.

Grooming

A Ragdoll's fur is easy to groom. It does not mat or tangle as easily as the fur of some other longhaired breeds. But you still need to brush your Ragdoll's coat once each week. You can use any type of brush, but a natural bristle brush works best. Plastic or other synthetic brushes can cause the cat's fur to stand on end from static electricity. A comb works well on thicker areas of a Ragdoll's coat.

You should brush your Ragdoll more often during spring. Ragdolls shed their winter coats at this time. Frequent brushings will help the cats get rid of loose hair.

Is a Ragdoll Right for You?

Ragdolls make good family pets. They get along well with dogs and other cats. Ragdolls' easygoing personalities help them fit in with busy families. They don't demand attention as often as some other breeds do. Ragdolls have few health problems and are generally easy to care for.

Visiting a breeder is one of the best ways to find a Ragdoll. Responsible breeders carefully select their cats for breeding. They make sure that the cats are healthy.

Adopting a cat is usually much less expensive than buying one from a breeder. You may be able to adopt a Ragdoll through a breed rescue organization or an animal shelter.

FUN FACT:
Ragdolls can live 15 years or more.

Siamese

Ask your friends to name a few cat breeds. Chances are that the Siamese will be included in their responses. Siamese cats are one of the best-known cat breeds in the world. People enjoy the Siamese for many reasons. Siamese are friendly, intelligent, and attractive cats that make excellent pets.

The Siamese breed has even received some attention in movies. In the 1950s, Peggy Lee and Sonny Burke wrote "The Siamese Cat Song" for the Disney company. Disney used it in the movie *Lady and the Tramp*.

The Siamese probably gets much of its popularity from its one-of-a-kind look. These cats have bold colorpoints and slanted blue eyes. A very slender, athletic body also sets them apart from other breeds.

FUN FACT: Siamese cats are very vocal. They are known for making a raspy yowl.

The colorpoints of the Siamese attract
many people to the breed.

Siamese History

The Siamese breed has a long history. People do not know exactly where the Siamese breed began. Siamese cats get their name from the eastern Asian region of Siam. Today this area is the country of Thailand.

In the 1500s, Siamese cats were sacred to the Siamese people. People believed that owning these cats brought good luck. Siamese cats may have lived as pets in Buddhist temples. People think the cats might have warned Buddhist priests of strangers approaching. Some cats also may have lived with the king of Siam.

Legend from the Past

Siamese cats of the past often had kinked tails and crossed eyes. These features no longer are common in the breed. But one of the most popular legends about Siamese cats describes how they got these features. According to the legend, two Siamese cats named Tien and Chula lived with a monk in a Buddhist temple. The monk was in charge of guarding a sacred cup.

One day the monk disappeared, and Tien left to search for a new monk. Chula stayed in the temple to guard the cup. Chula watched the cup for many days and began to grow tired. She decided to hook her tail around the cup so she could sleep. She knew that no one could take the cup from under her tail without waking her.

Finally, Tien returned with a new monk. Chula was still guarding the cup. But Chula's eyes were crossed from watching the cup for so long. Her tail was kinked from holding the cup. She had also given birth to kittens. The kittens were born with crossed eyes and kinked tails like Chula.

FUN FACT: The Siamese breed has been used to develop at least seven other cat breeds recognized by the CFA.

Siamese are popular for their striking blue eyes.

Cats of Royalty

While the story of Chula and Tien is a legend, there is no doubt that the Siamese breed has royalty in its roots. Siamese cats were important members of Siam's royal court. A Siamese cat was placed in the tomb of each dead king. Workers dug a hole in each tomb so the cat could escape.

When the cat came out, people believed the king's soul was inside the cat. The sacred cat then became part of the royal court. Its job was to watch over the new king. When the cat died, people believed it carried the dead king's soul into the afterlife.

Popularity Spreads Around the World

Officials from the British government came to Siam in the late 1800s. They had never seen a cat like the Siamese. Many British travelers brought Siamese cats home with them. At first many Europeans thought these cats were strange and ugly. But some people wanted to own the unusual cats.

In 1884 the king of Siam gave two Siamese cats named Pho and Mia to a British official. The cats became popular in Great Britain. In 1885 Pho and Mia had kittens. The kittens won prizes at the 1885 Crystal Palace cat show in London.

Siamese cats also made their way into the hearts of Americans in the late 1800s. In 1878 Rutherford B. Hayes was the U.S. president. Hayes' wife received a Siamese cat named Siam as a gift. The cat became sick and died a few months later. But Siam helped create interest in the breed in the United States. By the early 1900s, Siamese cats were appearing in U.S. cat shows.

FUN FACT: As recently as 1926, a Siamese cat was part of the coronation of the new king of Siam.

Since the early 1900s, Siamese have been popular at cat shows around the world.

The CFA officially recognized the
blue-point Siamese in 1934.

Siamese Traits

A Traditional Siamese

Today most Siamese cats look different from those of the past. In the past, Siamese had round heads. But modern Siamese have triangular, wedge-shaped heads. Today's Siamese also have larger ears and longer, more slender bodies than Siamese of the past. The CFA and some other registries allow only Siamese with this modern appearance in cat shows.

Body

Siamese are small-sized cats. Males are often larger than females. Males usually weigh between 8 and 10 pounds (3.6 and 4.5 kg). The average weight of females is between 5 and 7 pounds (2.3 and 3.2 kg).

Siamese cats' hips are about the same width as their shoulders. Even though the cats are slender, they have firm muscles. Long, slim legs match the cats' tubular bodies. A thin, **tapered** tail completes the graceful look of the Siamese.

Siamese have very short coats. The hair lies close to the body and has a glossy appearance.

FUN FACT: Some people still breed Siamese cats with round heads and sturdy bodies. These cats are called traditional or applehead Siamese.

Colors

The four original colors of Siamese cats are called classic Siamese colors. These colors occur naturally in the breed. They include seal point, chocolate point, blue point, and lilac point. The seal-point color is the best known. Seal-point cats have light coats with dark brown points. On some cats, the dark brown shade almost appears black. On a chocolate-point Siamese, the points are a lighter brown. The blue color looks like a shade of gray. Blue-point cats have blue-white bodies with blue points. Lilac-point Siamese have pink-gray points with white bodies.

Over time people have mated Siamese with other breeds. This breeding has produced **hybrid** Siamese with a variety of coat colors. These colors include tabby point and red point. Tabby-point Siamese have faintly striped coats and heavily striped points. Red-point Siamese have light bodies and red points.

The CFA allows only Siamese with classic colors to be shown. It considers Siamese without classic colors to be a separate breed called the Colorpoint Shorthair (page 191). Some other registries allow Siamese of all colors to be shown.

On a red-point Siamese, the shade of red can vary from faint to a dark orange-red color.

FUN FACT: Cats are **crepuscular**, which means they are most active at dawn and dusk. Has your cat ever tried to wake you up to play at the crack of dawn?

Siamese have athletic bodies that help them jump high.

What Causes Colorpoints?

A special gene in Siamese cats causes them to have colorpoints. This gene is heat-sensitive. Cool parts of the Siamese body have dark fur. Warm parts have light fur. All animals with this gene are born with white coats. The cooler parts of Siamese kittens' bodies turn dark when they are between 4 months and 1 year old. Fur on other parts of the body also may turn darker as the cat grows older.

Facial Features

The face of the modern Siamese is a big part of its unique look. Modern Siamese have wedge-shaped heads. The wedge starts at the nose and flares outward. The large ears of a Siamese are wide at the base and pointed at the tips.

All Siamese have blue eyes. The eyes are almond-shaped and slanted toward the nose.

Personality

Siamese are known for being social and loyal. They meow loudly to people as if they are talking to them. Siamese often bond closely with one person.

Siamese cats are also playful and intelligent. They seem to like games such as chasing and fetching balls. Some Siamese can be trained to do tricks or walk on a leash.

FUN FACT: The body parts where the point colors appear on a Siamese cat are cooler than the rest of the body. A Siamese in a cooler climate will have darker points than one in a warmer climate.

Caring for a Siamese

Health Care

The Siamese breed is strong and healthy. Siamese cats can live 15 years or more with good care.

There are no specific health problems linked to the Siamese breed. Some are born with crossed eyes or kinked tails, but these features don't affect a cat's health.

Like all cats, it is recommended by most rescue organizations and cat registries that you keep your Siamese indoors. Cats that are allowed to roam outside face dangers from cars and other animals. They are also more likely to develop diseases.

Grooming

Siamese have sleek coats that need little care. Only occasional brushing is needed to remove loose hair. Too much brushing can actually damage a Siamese's coat.

FUN FACT: Owners who show their Siamese often trim the hair inside the cats' ears. The trimming is done to make the ears appear larger.

Owning more than one cat will help keep
your Siamese from becoming bored.

Is a Siamese Right for You?

Siamese cats have friendly personalities. They seem to enjoy being around people and other animals. Siamese often make good pets for families with children, dogs, or other cats.

Siamese do not do well alone. They often seem unhappy without people or other animals to spend time with. Siamese owners who are not at home for long periods of time may want to adopt another cat. The two cats will be company for each other while the owners are away.

The best way to find a Siamese kitten is by visiting a breeder. Most breeders take steps to ensure the cats they sell are healthy. You can also adopt a Siamese through a breed rescue organization or an animal shelter.

With few health problems and a short, sleek coat, Siamese are relatively easy to care for. The rewards of owning a member of the intelligent, playful Siamese breed are many. By giving your Siamese good care, you'll be able to experience these rewards year after year.

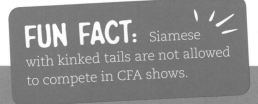

FUN FACT: Siamese with kinked tails are not allowed to compete in CFA shows.

Sphynx

Sphynx cats are one of the easiest cat breeds to spot because they have little hair on their bodies. Because of their lack of fur, the cats' other features stand out even more. They have wrinkled skin, large paws, and long toes. The cats also have large ears and wide, oval-shaped eyes.

Sphynx have muscular bodies and are active. But that doesn't mean they don't enjoy cuddling as well. They like to be around people, and they get along with other animals. They love attention and are happy playing with toys or curling up to their owners.

In 2016 the Sphynx was the eighth most popular breed in the CFA.

FUN FACT: Although most cats have wrinkled skin, Sphynx are known for having wrinkles because they don't have a fur coat covering their skin.

Sphynx are best known for their nearly hairless bodies.

Sphynx History

The Sphynx is one of the world's newest cat breeds. It was first recognized by cat registries in the 1960s. However, hairless cats have been around for a long time. Records of these cats began in the early 1900s. Around 1900 two hairless cats were born in New Mexico. The owners did not breed these cats because they were brother and sister. The cats were called New Mexican Hairless cats. Although they were similar in appearance to today's Sphynx, the two breeds are not related.

The Sphynx cat breed began by accident in 1966. A black and white pet cat in Ontario, Canada, gave birth to a hairless kitten. The owner named the kitten Prune because of its hairless, wrinkled skin. Prune's owner bred him to try to create more hairless kittens. Some of the resulting kittens had hair, while others were hairless.

The early hairless kittens had serious health problems. They did not develop proper **immune systems**. Cats' immune systems help protect them from diseases. Without immune systems, the cats were more likely to get sick or die. It was not safe to breed these cats because of the health risks. For a time, it looked like the breed would not continue.

FUN FACT: The Sphynx gets its name from the Great Sphinx statue in Giza, Egypt. This statue is 241 feet (73 meters) long and 66 feet (20 m) tall. It has the body of a lion and the face of a human.

Devon Rex cats were bred to hairless cats to create the Sphynx breed.

In 1978 three hairless kittens were found on the streets in Toronto, Canada. One kitten was male and two were female. The male kitten was named Bambi. The females were named Punkie and Paloma. Bambi stayed in Canada, but the two females were sent to a cat breeder in the Netherlands.

In 2002 the CFA accepted Sphynx in the main competitive classes at cat shows.

The breeder used Punkie and Paloma to begin a line of European Sphynx cats. The breeder mated the two females with a male Devon Rex, another cat breed with little body hair. Some offspring of these European Sphynx cats live in North America today.

Recognizing the Breed

The Sphynx breed had a tough time gaining recognition in the 1970s. Until about 1990, only TICA recognized the Sphynx. The cats could only appear at TICA shows.

Later other cat associations realized the Sphynx was becoming more popular. The associations wanted to include them in their shows as well. In 1998 the CFA recognized the Sphynx.

FUN FACT: Early on, some people called Sphynxes Canadian Hairless cats.

Sphynx Traits

Sphynx cats are small in size compared to other cat breeds. Most males weigh between 8 and 10 pounds (3.6 and 4.5 kg). Females are smaller. Most females weigh between 6 and 8 pounds (2.7 and 3.6 kg).

Body

Sphynx bodies fit with their playful and energetic nature. They have a sturdy frame, and their bodies are lean and muscular. They have strong tails that are long and tapered.

Facial Features

Sphynx cats have unique faces. They have a pointed face that is shaped like a wedge or an upside-down triangle. Because they have no fur, their faces look very narrow. Sphynx cats have long, wide ears and large, oval-shaped eyes.

Cats' whiskers are considered hairs. Sphynx do not have long, straight whiskers like most other cats do. Instead, the whiskers of a Sphynx are short and curly. Many do not have any whiskers at all.

FUN FACT: Since they lack the hair that other breeds have as insulation, Sphynx cats are always looking for warm places to cuddle and burrow.

The color of a Sphynx is determined by its skin.

Almost Hairless

Although Sphynx cats are sometimes called hairless cats, they do have some hair. Very short, fine hair called down covers the cats' bodies. The down may be slightly longer on the cats' ears, nose, tail, and paws. The down makes the Sphynx's body feel like a piece of **suede** or a warm peach.

A Sphynx's lack of body hair is the result of genes. Kittens receive some genes from the mother and some from the father. Genes give cats their eye color, body size, and gender.

Sphynx cats receive two genes that cause them to be hairless. They are called recessive genes and are weaker than other genes. Cats with furry coats sometimes carry one recessive gene for hairlessness. But they have another gene that gives them hair. Cats must receive a recessive hairless gene from each parent to be hairless.

Colors

Even though Sphynx cats are basically hairless, their skin can be many different colors. Some of these colors and color patterns include white, black, red, brown, calico, and tortoiseshell. Calico cats are white with patches of black and red. Tortoiseshell cats are a mixture of black and red with few or no white markings.

FUN FACT: The eyes of a Sphynx are lemon-shaped. The upper corners of the eyes point toward the ears.

Sphynx kittens receive their hairless genes from both parents.

Sphynx love to play with a variety of cat toys
and enjoy swatting at dangling objects.

Personality

Sphynx are friendly, intelligent cats. They are affectionate and enjoy being around children and animals. They seem to enjoy being the center of attention. If a Sphynx wants your attention, don't be surprised if it jumps into your lap or weaves between your legs. Sphynx are highly social cats. They have been known to greet their owners and even strangers at the door.

Sphynx cats are playful and energetic. They may tear up furniture or curtains if they become bored. Give your Sphynx cat toys or a cat tree to keep it busy.

If you're looking for a family pet, a Sphynx is a good choice. Sphynx seem to prefer homes with other pets to keep them company, particularly if they are left alone frequently. Owners who are often away from the house should consider getting two cats. Owners with two or more Sphynx cats should know that sometimes these cats enjoy traveling in packs.

The eyes of a Sphynx look especially big because of its lack of fur.

FUN FACT: Cats learn how owners react to specific sounds. They change the sound of their meow to get their needs met.

Caring for a Sphynx

Health Care

With proper care, Sphynx can live up to 15 years. Like other cats, the Sphynx should be kept indoors. Cats that roam outdoors are at a much greater risk of developing diseases than indoor cats. Outdoor cats also face dangers from cars and other animals.

Outdoor Sphynx cats face additional dangers. Because Sphynx have little hair, they have a hard time staying warm. The lack of fur also puts them at risk of being overexposed to the sun's rays. Without any fur, their skin could burn. Sphynx should be kept inside where the temperature is comfortable for them.

Sphynx cats no longer have problems with their immune systems like early hairless cats. But they can still become sick or inherit diseases. Breeders should have information on their cats' medical histories. If you buy your Sphynx from a breeder, you should review the cat's medical history. If you are planning to buy a kitten, it would be helpful to view its parents' medical histories.

Sphynx have fast **metabolisms**. Because of this fact it is especially important for them to be fed high-quality, nutritious food.

Grooming

Sphynx have little hair, but they still need to be groomed. Cats' coats often absorb the oils from their skin, but Sphynx coats can't do this job. Sphynx cats must be bathed about once every one to two weeks to keep their skin free of oils. Most pet stores sell special shampoo made for cats. The hard part will be getting your Sphynx in the tub.

FUN FACT: To make sure your house is at a good temperature for your Sphynx, use your own comfort as a guide. For example, if you're cold and need to bundle up in a blanket, your Sphynx is probably also cold.

Most cats don't like baths, but they usually enjoy being wrapped in a towel afterward.

Breeders should not sell kittens that are less than 12 weeks of age.

Cats usually do not like to be bathed. It is important to start bathing your Sphynx when it is a kitten. The kitten will then become used to taking baths. You should also rub your Sphynx with a damp, soft cloth every day to absorb body oil.

The Sphynx's ears require special care. The hair inside cats' ears usually helps keep out dirt and wax. But Sphynx's ears are hairless and very large. The insides of their ears often get dirty. Owners should wipe out their cats' ears with a soft, wet washcloth or a damp cotton ball every week.

Is a Sphynx Right for You?

People often believe that Sphynx cats make good pets for people who are **allergic** to cats. Some people who are allergic to cat hair can have a Sphynx as a pet. But Sphynx cats' skin still produces flakes called **dander**. People who are allergic to cat dander may still have an allergic reaction to Sphynx cats. If you are allergic to cats, you should spend some time around a Sphynx before getting one as a pet.

Sphynx cats are rare. Most animal shelters, breed rescue organizations, and pet stores do not have Sphynx available.

If you are interested in adopting a Sphynx, you should contact a breeder. Responsible breeders carefully breed their cats to make sure they are healthy.

Other Breeds

American Bobtail

Known to be experts at escaping enclosures, including closed rooms and cages, American Bobtail cats are playful problem-solvers. They are easily recognized by their short tails, which are approximately one-third to one-half the length of a typical cat's tail. The American Bobtail has a double coat, which helps protect it from rain and snow. These short-tailed cats are intelligent and affectionate.

American Curl

The distinguishing trait of the American Curl is its unusual ears, which are curled toward the back of its head. There are longhaired and shorthaired American Curls, and both shed little. American Curls are great pets for families with children. These cats are curious, playful, and friendly. They are able to adjust to new situations with ease. They enjoy physical affection, such as nuzzling their owners, and can often be found playing and exploring in their surroundings.

American Wirehair

The American Wirehair is a strong, muscular cat with a coat that feels like steel wool. The wirehair coat can consist of hairs that are crimped, curled, hooked, and bent. Wirehairs' whiskers are often textured as well. Like the American Curl, the Wirehair breed is known for being adaptable. This cat is people-focused and loves to play and purr!

Balinese

Offspring of the Siamese breed, Balinese cats stand out with their voluminous tails and long coat length. Balinese love to jump and climb. Like the Siamese, Balinese are happiest when interacting with humans. An intelligent breed, some people say that Balinese may even be able to tell the mood of humans, tending to stick close by if their owner is feeling down.

Bengal

Spots like a leopard and an athletic body make Bengal cats stand out from the crowd. The Bengal cat was originally a crossbreed — part Asian Leopard Cat and part domestic cat. Bengals are energetic and affectionate, though they are not lap cats. This cat has an impressive hunting ability, particularly when it comes to fish! They move like hunters too — sleek and quiet.

Bombay

With a sleek black coat and copper eyes, the Bombay was bred to look like a panther. These cats are easy going, sociable, and are easy to train. Some owners walk their Bombays on leashes or teach them to play fetch. Their round faces and eyes give Bombays a sweet appearance. Bombays enjoy the company of people and other animals and don't like to be left alone for too long.

Other Breeds

British Shorthair

The British Shorthair is a sturdy cat with a large, round head and wide eyes. Their coats can be almost any color or pattern, from solid to tricolor to tabby. British Shorthairs are known for their calm, quiet personalities. They are affectionate but don't demand attention from their owners. The British Shorthair may be descended from cats that traveled to the United Kingdom with Roman invaders about 2,000 years ago.

Burmese

This breed was developed by crossbreeding a small brown cat from Burma with Siamese cats in the United States. Favored for its solid brown coat color (known as sable) and its round head, this cat became recognized as a distinct breed by the CFA in 1936. Today there are four coat colors recognized by the CFA, including sable, blue, champagne, and platinum. Burmese love being around people, making them a good choice for families.

Burmilla

A relatively new cat breed, the Burmilla was originally part Burmese and part Chinchilla Persian. Its thick, silky coat lies close to its body. Characterized by its green eyes, the Burmilla has a sweet expression and a charming personality to match. They are curious and sociable and make great family pets. Though generally a healthy breed, some Burmillas are prone to allergies.

Chartreux

France's national cat has mysterious origins. Some people believe the Chartreux is the descendant of **feral** mountain cats, which were then brought to France and bred by monks. While the Chartreux has likely been in France for hundreds of years, it is a fairly new breed in the United States. The Chartreux breed became recognized by the CFA in 1987. A compact, sturdy cat with striking orange eyes and a thick, wooly gray coat, the Chartreux is also popular for its playful but quiet nature.

Colorpoint Shorthair

Perhaps the most vocal cat breed, the Colorpoint Shorthair is a busy and outgoing cat that demands a lot of attention from its owners. This breed was developed by breeding a Siamese and a red tabby American Shorthair. While this cat can have one of 20 different colorpoints, all Colorpoint Shorthairs have blue eyes. Since they don't produce a lot of dander, these cats are good pet options for people with allergies.

Cornish Rex

Hailing from Cornwall, Britain, the Cornish Rex has large ears and a sleek body covered in a fine, curly layer of down. Because the Cornish Rex doesn't have an outer coat to absorb natural oils, it needs to be bathed regularly. The Cornish Rex is an active and sturdy breed. These long and lean cats are known to enjoy games of fetch. Cornish Rex cats tend to have long lifespans. Some even live into their 20s!

Other Breeds

Devon Rex

Like the Cornish Rex, the Devon Rex is named after the area it came from — Devon, England. This medium-sized cat has a short, curly coat and a muscular body. Because of their thin coat, they give off more body heat than other cats. They can often be found seeking out heat sources on their own, from sunny windows to their owners' laps to the tops of refrigerators. Devon Rex cats are explorers. They enjoy aerial views, so don't be surprised if you find them climbing to the tops of doors or tall furniture.

Egyptian Mau

Egyptian Maus are known for their exotic appearance and their speed. This breed has a few distinct features. One of these features is a flap of skin that connects its flank to its hind leg. This feature allows Egyptian Maus great speed, flexibility, and agility. Another distinct physical trait is this cat's coat, which is spotted with a contrasting background color. Though they can be a bit shy around strangers, these cats often develop close relationships with their owners.

European Burmese

As indicated by its name, the European Burmese shares common ancestry with the Burmese breed. The European Burmese breed stands out with its array of coat colors. This cat has a slightly longer nose than its Burmese cousin, and its body is a bit leaner. Its big eyes are wide-set. In personality, the European Burmese is vocal, loyal, and loving.

Havana Brown

With a rich brown coat and striking green eyes, the Havana Brown is often described as a "Chocolate Delight." This breed tends to have sparse hair on parts of its face, including in front of the ears and just below the lower lip. Their heads are longer than they are wide, and they have large ears set far apart. Havana Browns are very curious, and they generally like to be involved in whatever their humans are doing.

Japanese Bobtail

Japanese Bobtails each have a distinct tail — no two tails are alike. The tail shape, size, direction, and composition varies greatly from one cat to another. The Japanese Bobtail's silky coat, which can be either longhair or shorthair, comes in many different colors including calico, solids, bi-colors, vans, and three different tabby patterns. A lover of its human friends, this cat has existed in Japan for several hundred years.

Korat

The Korat breed originated in Thailand, and references to this cat exist in literature dating back over 600 years. In Thai culture, this cat was thought to be an omen of good luck and prosperity. Korats have a blue-gray coat, distinct green eyes, and a muscular body. These active cats are especially sensitive to loud noises and sudden movements. Because of these heightened senses, they are best suited to a home with older children or adults.

Other Breeds

LaPerm

Due to a mutation, LaPerms have soft, curly coats that can be either longhaired or shorthaired. Like some other breeds, including the Maine Coon, LaPerms have tufts of hair that grow in their ears and on the tips of their ears. Equal parts explorer and lap cat, the LaPerm can adapt to many different lifestyles. The breed is an offshoot of Domestic Shorthairs and is generally very healthy.

Norwegian Forest Cat

In its homeland of Norway, the Norwegian Forest Cat is called "skoggkatt." This breed is relatively new to North America, but the skoggkatt has been recognized in Norway for centuries. Like the Maine Coon, the Norwegian Forest Cat is built to withstand harsh weather. Its waterproof double coat and tufted paws help protect it from ice, snow, and rain. A Norwegian Forest Cat may not reach its full size until age 5. These cats can range in weight from 9 to 16 pounds (4 to 7.2 kg).

RagaMuffin

Admired for its soft, beautiful coat, the RagaMuffin is medium to large in size. Females tend to range from 8 to 13 pounds (3.6 to 5.9 kg) and males from 14 to 20 pounds (6.4 to 9.1 kg). These calm, sweet cats develop deep bonds with their human families. They equally enjoy cuddling in their owners' laps and playing with toys. As its name suggests, this breed is related to the Ragdoll. Like the Ragdoll, RagaMuffins are also known for going limp when picked up.

Russian Blue

Russian Blues are shorthaired cats with dense gray-blue coats that seem to sparkle. The cat's origins are uncertain, but it is likely that the breed developed in Russia. Russian Blues tend to develop a close bond with one person and remain very loyal to that person. They can be shy around strangers, but they enjoy playtime with their owners — especially fetch!

Scottish Fold

Noted for its unusual ears, the Scottish Fold is unlike any other breed of cat recognized by the CFA. But this cat is not born this way. About three weeks after a litter is born, close to half of them will develop ears that fold down to the skull. The other half will have straight ears. These medium-sized cats have large, round eyes and round heads. There are shorthaired and longhaired Scottish Folds, and they come in a variety of colors.

Selkirk Rex

This curly-haired cutie can come from the same litter as kittens with straight hair. If a Selkirk Rex has curls at birth, its coat will be curly for the rest of its life. These cats often have kinked whiskers as well. Their plush, wooly coats can be either longhaired or shorthaired. A reserved and affectionate cat, the Selkirk Rex is soft to the touch. This relatively new breed was recognized by the CFA in 2000.

Other Breeds

Siberian

Though they first arrived in North America in 1990, Siberian cats have been revered in Russia for centuries. This breed has all the right physical traits to survive harsh winters in Siberia, including its thick, water-resistant coat, its furry tail, and its powerful, muscular body. These cats are quiet, playful, and friendly. They love toys, water, and being in the company of humans and other animals.

Singapura

True to its name, this small cat hails from the streets of Singapore. The Singapura has big ears and eyes and a short coat with a ticked brown pattern. Females are a bit smaller than males, but Singapura usually weigh in the range of 5 to 8 pounds (2.2 to 3.6 kg). The Singapura will want to be with their human friends as often as possible, and will remain people-oriented and playful throughout their lives.

Somali

A relative of the Abyssinian, the Somali has a medium-length agouti coat and a bushy tail. The four colors of Somali that are recognized by the CFA are red, ruddy, blue, and fawn. This breed is known for its enthusiastic, energetic, and outgoing personality. The Somali enjoys being active, whether it's finding small places to hide in or climbing to high perches. Some are even said to be able to open cupboards!

Tonkinese

The Tonkinese was produced by crossbreeding Siamese and Burmese. Its coat comes in a variety of colors, patterns, and markings. These mischievous cats don't like to be left alone. Tonkinese need plenty of attention, toys, and scratching posts to keep them entertained and out of trouble. They are often looking to socialize and will happily greet visitors at the door.

Turkish Angora

This striking cat comes from the mountains of Turkey. Its long coat comes in many colors and patterns including black, white, blue, red, and cream. While the Turkish Angora's coat isn't prone to matting, this cat needs to be groomed more often in warmer months. Turkish Angoras are known to be clever, outgoing, and loving, but if you are looking for a lap cat, an Angora is probably not the right choice. These kitties like their independence!

Turkish Van

A rare breed, Turkish Van cats didn't arrive in the U.S. until 1982, but they have existed in parts of Europe and the Middle East for centuries. Turkish Vans love water. Some may even try to hop in the bathtub with you! This cat can grow to be quite large (up to 18 pounds, or 8.2 kg), though some cats won't reach full physical maturity until age 5. Turkish Vans tend to have a lot of energy, and they like to be up high where they can view all the action.

Care Tips

Health Care

Most veterinarians recommend yearly visits for cats. Older cats may need to visit the vet two or three times each year. Cats tend to have more health problems as they get older. More frequent checkups help vets treat these issues early.

At a typical checkup, the vet will check the cat's heart, lungs, eyes, ears, and mouth. At your cat's first checkup, ask the vet about which **vaccinations** your cat needs. Cats should receive vaccinations to protect against diseases such as **rabies** and **feline leukemia**. Cats can also be vaccinated against several respiratory diseases that cause breathing or lung problems. Kittens often receive their first vaccinations when they are about 10 weeks old.

Rabies is a deadly disease that is spread by animal bites. Many states have laws that require owners to vaccinate their cats against rabies. Feline leukemia attacks a cat's immune system. Cats with this disease are unable to fight off infections and other illnesses. Cats should receive some vaccinations each year, while other vaccinations are given less often.

Vets can also spay and neuter cats. These surgeries make it impossible for cats to breed. You should have your cat spayed or neutered if you don't plan to breed it. There are many animals that don't have homes, and these surgeries help control pet populations. According to the American Humane Society, between 6 and 8 million cats and dogs enter animal shelters each year in the United States. Unspayed female cats can have three or four litters of kittens each year. Spaying and neutering your pets will also help protect them from certain diseases. Another benefit of these surgeries is that spayed and neutered cats usually have calmer personalities than cats that do not have the surgeries.

Many animal humane organizations recommend keeping your cat indoors at all times. Outdoor cats are at a much greater risk of developing diseases and acquiring parasites. They also are exposed to dangers such as cars, severe weather, other animals, and toxic substances. Furthermore, cats can cause a lot of damage to their environments when left outdoors, including killing birds, rodents, and other small animals.

Cats sometimes inherit diseases such as cardiomyopathy from their parents. Cardiomyopathy is a serious heart disease. Responsible cat breeders test their animals for inherited diseases. They will not breed animals that can pass along serious illnesses. But if your cat does develop an inherited disease, your vet can identify and treat it.

Some cats develop a condition called chin acne. A cat with this condition has crusty black patches on its chin. Both food allergies and plastic food bowls can cause chin acne. Owners can help prevent chin acne by putting their cats' food and water in stainless steel or glass bowls.

Care Tips

Dental Care

Cats need regular dental care to protect their teeth and gums from plaque. Brushing your cat's teeth once a week will help prevent gum diseases, such as gingivitis, and tooth decay.

Use a special toothbrush made for cats or a soft cloth. Make sure you always use toothpaste that is made for cats.

Nail Care

Nail trimming helps reduce damage if cats claw furniture, and it protects cats from infections and pain caused by ingrown nails. A cat with ingrown nails has claws that have grown into the bottom of the paw. Cats can get ingrown nails if their nails are not trimmed regularly.

It is best to begin trimming a cat's nails when it is a kitten. Cats should have their nails trimmed every few weeks. You can purchase a nail trimmer made for cats at a pet store. These tools are easy to handle and reduce the risk of injury to your cat.

Some people take their cats to the veterinarian to be **declawed**. These permanent surgeries either remove part of the claw or keep a cat from **retracting** the claw. But declawing can cause cats pain. It also puts the cats at risk if they get outdoors. They are less able to hunt and defend themselves. The CFA and other organizations disapprove of declawing.

Grooming

Depending on the length and texture of your cat's hair, you may have to groom your cat once a day, once a week, or less often.

Cats' fur sometimes clumps together in mats. You should never cut out mats with scissors. Using scissors can injure the cat's skin and damage its fur. Instead, bring your cat to a veterinarian or a professional groomer.

Feeding

All cats need a balanced, nutritious diet. Both dry and moist food are suitable. Dry food usually is less expensive. Eating dry food helps clean a cat's teeth. Dry food will not spoil if it is left out. Moist food can spoil easily and should not be left out for more than one hour.

The amount of food needed depends on your cat's size and appetite. You can use the feeding instructions on the package as a guide. A veterinarian can also help you decide how much to feed your cat. Some owners feed both dry and moist food to their cats. This variety can help keep a cat from becoming bored with its diet. Some owners **free feed** their cats by filling their dishes with dry food and allowing their cats to eat throughout the day. Putting out a specific amount of food will ensure that your cat won't overeat.

Owners should make sure their cats' water bowls are always filled. Cats need to drink plenty of water to stay healthy. You should change the water each day to keep it clean.

Care Tips

Scratching Posts

Cats like to scratch — and need to scratch — for a variety of reasons. When cats sharpen their claws on scratching posts, the old part of the nail falls off. They mark their territories by leaving their scent on objects they scratch. They also scratch to release tension and to stretch their bodies and flex their paws. You should provide your cat with a scratching post so that it won't scratch the carpet, furniture, or curtains.

You can buy a scratching post at a pet store. Many scratching posts are covered with a strong rope called **sisal**, which won't shred when your cat sharpens its claws on it. Sisal is also a more satisfying material for your cat to scratch, as opposed to softer surfaces such as couches and curtains. Another option is to ask an adult to help you make a scratching post out of wood and carpet.

Litter Box

Cats also need to have a litter box. The litter box should be large enough so your cat can move around and easily get in and out. A good rule for the number of litter boxes to provide is one for each cat you have, plus one extra.

Most litter is made of clay, but it can also be made out of wood, wheat, or corn. When you fill the litter box, the litter should be 2 to 3 inches (5 to 7.6 cm) deep. Remember to clean the waste out of the box each day. You should also change the litter often, preferably at least once every two weeks. Some cats may refuse to use a dirty litter box. It is a good idea to put your cat's litter box in a different area from her food and water. Some cats may also refuse to use a litter box that is placed too close to their food and water bowls.

Exercise

Some cats need a lot of exercise each day to keep them stimulated and entertained. Others may prefer to just lounge on the couch. Most will like to do both! There are many ways to keep your cat happy and active, including providing him plenty of toys. Cats also like to climb, hide, and watch wildlife. Consider setting out cardboard boxes or paper bags for your cat to hide in. Cat trees and climbing posts are a good way for your cat to get up off the ground. Another option for cat entertainment is to place a bird feeder or birdbath outside of a window in your home. Your cat will love to watch them! If you do put in a birdbath or feeder, just make sure never to let your cat outside. Cats have strong hunting instincts, even if they are well fed.

Glossary

agouti (uh-GOO-tee)—a coat that has bands of light and dark color on each hair; an agouti coat is sometimes called a ticked coat

allergic (a-LUHR-jik)—having a reaction to certain things such as pollen, dust, or animals

arthritis (ahr-THRYE-tis)—a disease in which joints become swollen and painful

bacteria (bak-TEER-ee-uh)—very small living things that can be found in nature; many bacteria are useful, but some cause disease

breed (BREED)—a certain kind of animal within an animal group; breed also means to mate and raise a certain kind of animal

breed standard (BREED STAN-durd)—certain physical features in a breed that judges look for at a cat show

cardiomyopathy (CAR-dee-oh MYE-ah-pah-thee)—a serious heart disease that results in poor heart function

cartilage (KAHR-tuh-lij)—a strong, rubbery tissue that connects bones in most animals

colorpoint (KUHL-ur-point)—a pattern in which the ears, face, tail, and legs are darker than the base color

compact (kuhm-PAKT)—short-bodied, solid, and without excess flesh

crossbreed (kros-BREED)—to mix one breed with another breed

crepuscular (kri-PUS-kyoo-luhr)—active during twilight

dander (DAN-duhr)—skin flakes in an animal's fur or hair

declawed (DEE-clawd)—permanent surgeries that either remove part of a cat's claw or keep a cat from retracting the claw

deformity (di-FORM-it-ee)—being twisted, bent, or disfigured

descendant (di-SEN-duhnt)—an animal's offspring and family members born to those offspring

diabetes (dye-uh-BEE-teez)—a disease in which there is too much sugar in the blood

domesticated (duh-MES-ti-kay-tid)—no longer wild; people keep domesticated animals as pets

fawn (FAWN)—a light brown color

feline leukemia (FEE-line loo-KEE-mee-uh)—a disease that attacks a cat's immune system, making the cat unable to fight off infections and other illnesses

feral (FARE-uhl)—not domesticated

flank (FLANGK)—the side of an animal's body between the ribs and the hip

free feed (FREE FEED)—to leave out food for a cat, allowing it to eat when it wants

gene (JEEN)—a part of every cell that carries physical and behavioral information passed from parents to their offspring

gingivitis (jin-juh-VYE-tuhss)—an inflammation of the gums

hairball (HAIR-bawl)—a ball of fur that lodges in a cat's stomach

hazel (HAY-zuhl)—a green-brown color

hybrid (HYE-brid)—the offspring of two different breeds

immune system (i-MYOON SIS-tuhm)—the system that protects a living animal's body against disease and infection

inherit (in-HAIR-it)—to receive a characteristic from parents

insulin (IN-suh-luhn)—a substance made in the pancreas that helps the body use sugar

litter (LIT-ur)—a number of baby animals that are born at the same time to a mother; also, small bits of clay or other material used to absorb the waste of cats

mat (MAT)—to form into a tangled mass

metabolism (muh-TAB-uh-liz-uhm)—the rate at which food changes into energy

mitted (MIT-ed)—a color pattern that includes white foot markings and white on the stomach, chin, and chest

mouser (MAUS-er)—a cat that is good at catching mice and rats

mutation (myoo-TAY-shun)—a change in an animal's genes that results in a new characteristic or trait

native (NAY-tiv)—a person, an animal, or a plant that originally lived or grew in a certain place

overweight (OH-vur-wate)—above a normal or desirable weight

pedigreed (PED-i-gree)—a cat that is pedigreed has a recorded ancestry that shows it to be purebred

perch (PURCH)—to sit or stand on the edge of something, often high up

plaque (PLAK)—the coating of food, saliva, and bacteria that forms on teeth and can cause tooth decay

prey (PRAY)—an animal hunted by another animal for food

proportion (pruh-POR-shuhn)—the relation of one part to another; an animal has good proportion is when a body part doesn't seem too large or too small in comparison to another

purebred (PYOOR-bred)—having ancestors of the same breed or kind of animal

rabies (RAY-bees)—a deadly disease that is spread by animal bites

registry (REH-juh-stree)—an organization that keeps track of the ancestry for cats of certain breeds

renal amyloidosis (REE-nuhl am-uh-loy-DOH-suhss)—a disease that causes kidney failure and death in cats

reproduce (ree-pruh-DOOSE)—to breed and have offspring

retract (ree-TRAKT)—to draw back in

ruddy (RUH-dee)—having a reddish color

ruff (RUHF)—long hairs growing around an animal's neck

seal-point (SEEL-POINT)—a coat pattern in which the colorpoints are very dark brown

sebum (SEE-buhm)—an oily liquid produced by the skin glands

sisal (SYE-zuhl)—a strong rope made from a plant of the same name

tabby (TAB-ee)—a striped coat

tapered (TAY-purd)—to be more narrow at one end than the other

ticked (TIKT)—a coat pattern that has light and dark bands of color on each hair

trait (TRATE)—a quality or characteristic that makes one person or animal different from another

vaccination (vak-suh-NAY-shun)—a shot of medicine that protects animals from disease

van (VAN)—a white coat with a colored tail and splashes of color between the ears

wedge (WEDG)—a shape like an upside-down triangle

Index

Photo Credits

The Cat Encyclopedia for Kids is published by
Capstone Young Readers, A Capstone Imprint
1710 Roe Crest Drive, North Mankato, Minnesota 56003
www.mycapstone.com

Library of Congress Cataloging-in-Publication Data
is available on the Library of Congress website.

ISBN: 978-1-62370-937-2 (paperback)
ISBN: 978-1-62370-939-6 (reflowable epub)

Previously published as twelve library-bound editions:
ISBN: 978-1-4296-6628-2 ISBN: 978-1-4296-6629-9
ISBN: 978-1-4296-6630-5 ISBN: 978-1-4296-6631-2
ISBN: 978-1-4296-6632-9 ISBN: 978-1-4296-6633-6
ISBN: 978-1-4296-6634-3 ISBN: 978-1-4296-6635-0
ISBN: 978-1-4296-6636-7 ISBN: 978-1-4296-6865-1
ISBN: 978-1-4296-6866-8 ISBN: 978-1-4296-6867-5

Editorial Credits
Carly J. Bacon, Angie Peterson Kaelberer, Rebecca Rissman,
and Maureen Webster, contributing authors;
Eliza Leahy, editor; Tracy McCabe, designer;
Morgan Walters, media researcher;
Tori Abraham, production specialist

Printed and bound in the United States of America.
11035R